The Pastoral Head's Handbook

JEFF JONES
MAZDA JENKIN
JIM ANDREWS

Heinemann Educational Publishers
Halley Court, Jordan Hill, Oxford OX2 8EJ
a division of Reed Educational & Professional Publishing Ltd

OXFORD MELBOURNE AUCKLAND
JOHANNESBURG BLANTYRE GABORONE
IBADAN PORTSMOUTH (NH) USA CHICAGO

Heinemann is a registered trademark of Reed Educational & Professional
Publishing Ltd

Text © Jeff Jones, Mazda Jenkin, Jim Andrews, 1999

First published 1999

03 02
10 9 8 7 6 5

British Library Cataloguing in Publication Data
A catalogue record for this book is available from the British Library

ISBN 0 435 80054 X

Typeset by 🖌 Tek-Art, Croydon Surrey
Printed and bound in Great Britain by Athenaeum Press Ltd., Gateshead

Authors' acknowledgements
The authors wish to express their sincere thanks to the many colleagues in a
large number of schools whose professionalism and expertise has
contributed to the writing of this book.

Contents

Introduction

Our purpose in writing *The Pastoral Head's Handbook* is to offer you and your team support in fulfilling a vitally important role. As a Pastoral Head (Head of Year/House/Section) you have a key middle-management role within your school. Traditionally, the role has been concerned mainly with pupil discipline, but recent legislation and public concern about issues such as bullying, together with a trend towards seeing effective whole-school pastoral care as an essential support for pupils' learning, has broadened the role and made Pastoral Heads aware of the need to develop a range of management skills. We hope that this very practical book, based on the experience of the writers and the many schools whose practice has informed their work, will offer the support and guidance to help you define and carry out your role.

The handbook is not prescriptive, but is intended to be of practical help to both existing and aspiring Pastoral Heads in fully understanding the managerial aspects of your role. Above all, it should act as a stimulus for you in organising your thoughts and developing your strategy for school improvement.

Jeff Jones   Principal Lecturer, School of Education, University of Wolverhampton

Mazda Jenkin   Headteacher, Rising Brook High School, Stafford

Jim Andrews   Educational Consultant; previously Headteacher, Evesham High School, Worcestershire

1 The role of the Pastoral Head

Introduction

As with the rest of education, the role of the Pastoral Head is undergoing change. As Michael Marland says:

'The pastoral responsibility has long been defined as the core of the work of a school, enabling the child to develop as a student and an individual. In the past many people perhaps regarded it as mainly concerned with discipline, but for some time now it has been clearly seen that effective whole-school pastoral care is an essential support for pupils' learning. The over-arching aims of the Education Reform Act 1988 and the government's and QCA's emphasis on Personal, Social and Health Education has re-emphasised the broader role.' (Marland, 1998)

The development of the school improvement and school effectiveness movements have again highlighted the importance of pastoral care to support pupils' learning.

'Pastoral Heads are now even more aware of the need to develop a range of management skills.' (Marland, 1998)

Whether a Head of Year, Head of House or Head of a section within a school (e.g. lower school or upper school), the Pastoral Head, like a Head of Faculty or Department, is a middle manager upon whom much responsibility rests. Middle-management roles can be challenging and require both commitment and professionalism.

Pastoral Heads must be particularly sure that they have these qualities, given that some of the pupils they work with will test them severely.

Perhaps the first and most important thing to say about the role is what it is not! Many teachers gain promotion to the post of Pastoral Head on the basis of effective discipline, both as a classroom teacher and as a tutor. It is for this reason that the position is far more likely to be an internal appointment than that of a Head of Department. Of course, effective discipline is essential, but Pastoral Heads should never allow themselves to be marginalised into a purely 'policing' role or into acting as 'enforcers' on behalf of other colleagues. The narrow view of the role, unfortunately still held by some, will quickly demoralise even the most dedicated and optimistic and must be resisted at all costs.

The role of the Pastoral Head is not always clearly spelt out or understood. Pastoral Heads need to see their role as proactively as possible, therefore minimising the need solely to react to incidents. For this to happen, Pastoral Heads should pay particular attention to the following elements of their role:

- their contribution to, and monitoring of, the quality of teaching and learning
- the nature of the relationships amongst pupils, teachers and other adults
- monitoring all pupils' overall welfare, performance and progress
- the management of pupil behaviour
- the pastoral curriculum as a means of articulating school values etc.
- leadership of the pastoral team
- policy formulation, monitoring and evaluation
- the range, appropriateness and benefits of extra-curricular activities
- ways of promoting pupils' spiritual, moral, social and cultural development.

The role in context

Above all else the Pastoral Head is leader of a team which reaches out into the community beyond the school's gates. The welfare and progress of all pupils is the responsibility of all teachers, both as classroom teachers and as tutors, but it is the Pastoral Head who carries the overall responsibility and is at the heart of major developments as well as problems, as and when they arise.

The role of the Pastoral Head needs to be seen in the context of your school's:

- values
- beliefs
- expectations
- aims.

As you contemplate the values underlying your pastoral care system you may find it helpful to consider the following list offered by the National Association for Pastoral Care in Education (NAPCE). The Pastoral Head should:

- provide a point of personal contact with every pupil
- provide a point of personal contact with parents
- monitor pupil progress across the curriculum
- provide support and guidance for pupil achievement
- encourage a caring and orderly environment
- promote a school which meets pupils' needs
- provide colleagues with information to adapt teaching
- engage wider networks as appropriate.

The following example of a job description is also included in the Resource Bank at the back of the book (RB1).

Sample job description

POST: Head of Year

Under the general direction of the Headteacher, the Year Head has responsibility for the pastoral care and academic progress of a cohort of students. He/she therefore has the following duties and responsibilities:

1 To get to know students in the year group as well as possible and to become accepted as a person to whom they can turn for guidance in addition to their form tutor.

2 To monitor the progress of students. To insist on high standards of co-operation and behaviour and to initiate action when these are unsatisfactory, using strategies such as the Year Heads' Report System, counselling, detention, etc. School policy requires that parents are involved in pastoral and disciplinary matters at an early stage.

3 In discussion with form tutors, Head of Careers and Deputy Heads, to direct and organise a programme of tutorial work for students.

4 To be a member of the Year Heads' Committee and to work with the Senior Management Team to develop appropriate policies and procedures for the effective pastoral care of all students.

5 To lead a team of form tutors, ensuring through regular minuted meetings that all members of the team understand the policies of the school as well as making the Senior Management Team aware of the tutors' views and of the tutor teams' ideas for development. Proposals may be placed on the Year Heads' Agenda for consideration across the whole school.

6 To ensure, by attendance at meetings and regular briefings, that the Headteacher and members of the Senior Management Team are kept informed of matters pertaining to the year group, academic progress, co-operation, attendance, etc.

7 To co-ordinate all information received from staff, parents and outside agencies regarding individual students. To ensure this information is distributed correctly and to check that action is taken where and when necessary.

8 To be responsible for the maintenance of appropriate records, including students' individual files, and to ensure that these are passed on when students transfer.

9 To organise the preparation of reports, records of achievement and references, including confidential court/social service/medical reports.

10 To participate in liaison arrangements with other phases of the student's education, contributory Middle Schools, Year 12/13 and Further Education colleges.

11 To be responsible for the operation of the school's Special Needs Code of Practice as it pertains to behavioural aspects, including appropriate documentation, liaison with SENCO and the Deputy Head with responsibility for Learning Support.

Skills and qualities needed

Because of its complexity, pastoral care places very special demands on managers to provide supportive structures for helping pupils cope with the ever-increasing pressures upon them. As a new Pastoral Head, you will need to make the transition from your present position to your role as a manager, with responsibilities ranging from planning and implementation to monitoring and evaluation. The role has four key aspects:

Leadership

- by creating a shared vision and an ethos of co-operation and achievement
- by establishing productive tutor periods, extra-curricular activities, etc.
- by designing and implementing a pastoral curriculum which promotes social development, increases motivation (e.g. through careers advice and action planning) and raises aspirations.

Monitoring

- of academic performance, through liaison with colleagues and parents and through a monitoring role in the school's reporting system
- of attendance, punctuality, co-operation, behaviour and achievement.

Support and guidance

- for pupils, their welfare and protection, guidance and counselling
- for team members and other colleagues, ensuring consistency of care across all groups of pupils.

Administration

- liaison with other phases of education (primary, secondary, tertiary) and professionals and with parents
- oversight of systems for recording and reporting progress, records of achievement, references and the Code of Practice in relation to behavioural problems affecting learning
- effective communication
- efficient use of time for facilitating the work of the team.

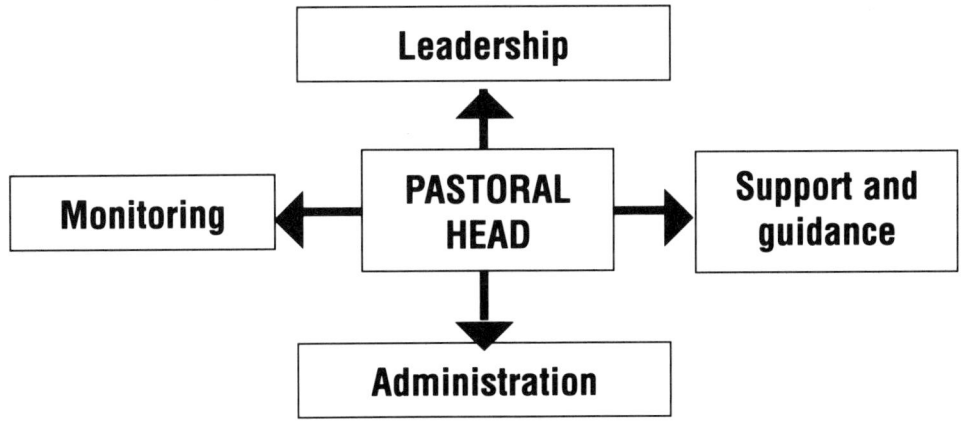

Dilemmas and pitfalls

Such a complex and far-reaching role can lead to some traditional dilemmas and pitfalls, so it is just as well to be aware of them now rather than later. These include:

1 The expectation of other colleagues that the Pastoral Head can deal with all the discipline problems in the year single-handedly.

Some Pastoral Heads fall willingly into this heroic role and enjoy the recognition and kudos associated with dealing successfully with troublesome pupils. However, unless the classroom-based issues are also dealt with – and this can include the poor teaching of colleagues – success can be an illusion, with the pupil behaving well for the Pastoral Head but not modifying his/her behaviour in the classroom. All staff need to be involved in the creation and maintenance of good behaviour and the Pastoral Head should avoid creating the impression that he/she alone can solve what are sometimes complex issues.

2 A lack of clarity regarding the boundaries of responsibility with academic staff.

This lack of clarity often comes to the fore when poor pupil behaviour stems from an inappropriate curriculum or inadequate teaching. Whose responsibility is it to deal with this situation? Is it the appropriate Pastoral Head, the Head of Department or a member of the senior team? Some Pastoral Heads' roles include a specific curriculum function, e.g. curriculum liaison at the point of transition. Since this serves to support learning it is important that any confusion regarding the roles occupied by Pastoral Heads and subject leaders are dealt with effectively.

3 Absence of a culture of pastoral development.

Schools often expect the curriculum to change and put in place plans to monitor such changes. However, pastoral care is too often thought of as a static area – one in which new ideas or approaches are not expected or sought.

Evaluating your performance and future needs

As a new Pastoral Head you are likely to possess many of the necessary skills and qualities to meet the challenge of providing effective pastoral care for a group of pupils. It is possible to develop others through experience, observation and in-service training.

ACTIVITY

A useful starting point for considering your own development needs is to evaluate your current performance using the questionnaire below. It could form the basis of your personal development plan, which you should discuss with your school's Professional Development Co-ordinator. Rate your performance using the following scale:

1 = very good; 2 = good; 3 = satisfactory; 4 = some weaknesses; 5 = area for improvement.

Be honest – but don't underestimate your abilities!

	1	2	3	4	5
1 Ability to communicate with members of the pastoral team	☐	☐	☐	☐	☐
2 Ability to communicate ideas in writing	☐	☐	☐	☐	☐
3 Ability to communicate ideas orally	☐	☐	☐	☐	☐
4 Ability to represent the views of the pastoral team to SMT	☐	☐	☐	☐	☐

		1	2	3	4	5
5	Ability to represent the views of SMT to the pastoral team	☐	☐	☐	☐	☐
6	Ability to organise the administration of pastoral care	☐	☐	☐	☐	☐
7	Ability to delegate responsibilities to others within the team	☐	☐	☐	☐	☐
8	Ability to listen to the views of pupils and staff	☐	☐	☐	☐	☐
9	Ability to influence and motivate pupils	☐	☐	☐	☐	☐
10	Ability to chair pastoral team meetings	☐	☐	☐	☐	☐
11	Ability to handle difficult members of the team	☐	☐	☐	☐	☐
12	Ability to provide constructive criticism	☐	☐	☐	☐	☐
13	Ability to accept constructive criticism	☐	☐	☐	☐	☐
14	Ability to plan ahead and set realistic targets for pastoral development	☐	☐	☐	☐	☐
15	Ability to implement agreed plans	☐	☐	☐	☐	☐
16	Ability to solve problems	☐	☐	☐	☐	☐
17	Ability to use time effectively	☐	☐	☐	☐	☐
18	Ability to manage stress	☐	☐	☐	☐	☐
19	Ability to identify priorities	☐	☐	☐	☐	☐
20	Ability to understand whole-school issues	☐	☐	☐	☐	☐

A copy of this checklist is included in the Resource Bank (RB2). Use the outcomes of this questionnaire to start to write your personal development plan. In the example shown below a Pastoral Head has used the questionnaire to identify areas for personal development.

Extract from Pastoral Head's personal development plan

Area for development	Targets	INSET required
Chairing meetings	■ circulate agenda prior to meeting ■ ensure everyone has a say ■ summarise agreements ■ keep meeting to time	Course, video or discussion with Professional Development Co-ordinator
Listening skills	■ ask open questions ■ don't interrupt ■ avoid imposing solutions ■ consider your own body language	Course on counselling

Whether or not you make use of this approach, it is important to keep your own development needs under review. You will want to keep up to date with the latest research into pastoral areas of concern such as bullying, truancy, disaffection, new legislation in these and allied areas, as well as developing your skills as a manager.

It is easy for Pastoral Heads to get totally involved in the daily life of the school, but it is important to remain open to, and interested in, ideas from colleagues in other schools and also ideas from other professionals (e.g. from advisory/inspectorial services, consultancies and higher education). Attending cluster meetings, INSET or undertaking further professional study (e.g. a distance-learning MA) can enhance your effectiveness and broaden your knowledge and understanding. You may also wish to consider the development possibilities in your own school. A great deal can be gained from working with other staff in whole-school initiatives (e.g. the provision of in-house INSET, chairing a working party looking at the improvement of boys' attitudes towards learning, or on the improvement of literacy levels).

2 Leading the pastoral team

Introduction

No less than the Head of Department or Faculty, the Pastoral Head is the leader of a team and cannot operate without the support and commitment of that team. Happily, the 'I'm a teacher of Mathematics, not a social worker' school of thought is less prevalent these days. However, Pastoral Heads will continue to face team members whose first commitment will not be to pastoral care but to their subject discipline. Although some new teachers entering the profession have received some training in the area of the pastoral curriculum and the responsibilities of tutors, others have not. This situation presents a challenge for Pastoral Heads who may have to impart the concepts of pastoral care and the principles underlying a pastoral curriculum.

The pastoral team

As is often the case with other management activities, the pastoral work of the school is most effectively accomplished with and through teams. In their middle-management role Pastoral Heads should attempt to:

- provide leadership
- maintain morale

- encourage staff development
- facilitate co-operation between staff.

Staff working in partnership have the potential to:

- identify the needs of pupils more effectively
- contribute information which is relevant to pupils' learning.

The characteristics of effective teamwork

Effective teamwork is characterised by:

- clear goals and direction
- openness
- support and trust
- co-operation
- clearly thought out procedures
- appropriate leadership
- regular review
- individual development
- sound inter-group relations.

Team building

Team building is a valuable management tool especially given the potentially diverse group of tutors that the Pastoral Head has to transform into a team. Groups develop into teams when their common purpose is understood by all of the members. This enables each member to play an assigned role using her/his skills to best advantage. Good team leaders are able to integrate their individual skills to accentuate strengths and minimise weaknesses in order to achieve team objectives.

Team leaders exhibit varying styles – styles that are often shaped by experience and the values adopted over the years. To remain effective as a team leader it is important to re-evaluate and modify your style on a regular basis.

To build an effective team:
- hold regular team meetings and work to an agenda to which team members have been given the opportunity to contribute. Ensure

that brief minutes or action notes are kept and circulated to all members so that everyone is clear on policies and procedures. Tea and biscuits will help create the right atmosphere!

- encourage tutors to do things with their groups and together, rotate responsibility for tasks (e.g. leading assemblies, tidying a social area, looking after notice-boards, etc.)
- encourage tutors to take responsibility for aspects relating to the whole cohort (e.g. chairing student council, organising the school photographs, sports and competitions, etc.). This will bring them into contact with other tutors and groups, making for greater coherence and an ethos of teamwork
- invite team members to talk about aspects of their work as tutors (e.g. as a regular agenda item at team meetings), particularly where you know they have strengths. This sharing of good practice will enhance the tutor's self-esteem and commitment and develop the ethos of teamwork. More importantly, it will contribute to your prime objective of encouraging coherence and consistency amongst tutors and thus ensure that all pupils have access to similar experiences and level of support
- lead by example but don't accept this to mean that you do all the work! Your job is to lead and co-ordinate a team who are jointly responsible for the welfare of a group of pupils. Don't wait for tutors to offer to take on particular jobs – be direct and ask them. If you have a team of eight, make up a list of ten jobs that need doing. Take on two of them yourself and ask each member of your team to undertake one. Most will accept cheerfully, making it difficult for the less willing to refuse
- monitor tutor performance and feedback. Give figures, by tutor group, on attendance, punctuality, behaviour referrals, etc. A good Pastoral Head will know the circumstances in which allowances should be made but will also know where tutor performance is falling short of the mark. Even apparently inconsequential data, such as returns of school funds, photograph money, trip consent forms, etc. are usually accurate indications of the effectiveness of the tutor's relationship with pupils and the morale of the group
- arrange opportunities for observing tutorial sessions. You will not normally have a teaching commitment during tutorial time. Over a

period of a few weeks you can arrange to join a tutorial session with each tutor in turn. This allows the sharing of good practice and support for the less confident. Also, by taking over a session with each form, you can release colleagues for observation whilst at the same time monitoring the quality of the tutorial work in each group.

ACTIVITY

What kind of team leader are you?

Ask yourself the following questions:

- Have I allocated the tutor groups fairly?
- Have I delegated routine duties, chores, creative tasks and projects appropriately?
- Have I allowed some scope for tutors to be creative/ independent decision-makers?
- Does each tutor have a clear description of his/her role?
- Do I know the strengths, weaknesses, concerns and aspirations of my tutors?
- Is there opportunity for regular individual review?
- Do I discuss with each tutor her/his professional development/INSET requirements?
- Do I balance individual needs against the needs of the whole team?
- Have I set achievable targets for the year?
- Do I consult with the team and accept their advice?
- Do I keep the team fully informed?
- How well do I explain their case to the Senior Management Team?
- Do they have adequate resources to carry out their tasks?
- How well have I presented my personal/the school's philosophy to the team?

Your answers to these questions will help you to prioritise and plan your development within the role. A copy of this checklist is included in the Resource Bank at the end of this book (RB3).

Dealing with administration

Apart from the care of groups of pupils, the role of the Pastoral Head also includes more than its fair share of administration. For example, record keeping and filing. Well-organised schools have recognised the administrative burden on Pastoral Heads and have provided an element of clerical support for the more routine tasks. In other schools it may be necessary to work with senior managers and other pastoral staff to review administrative support arrangements.

Administration can occupy much of your time and, in relation to individual tasks, it is helpful to consider:

- does this task need to be done at all?
- when does this task need to be undertaken?
- when does it need to be completed?
- what is the most efficient way of handling it?
- who should undertake this task?
- does completion of this task support students in their learning?

The following is a list of routine administrative tasks carried out by many or all Pastoral Heads. Think carefully about these tasks; you may want to involve others, including form tutors.

- Keeping records of pupil misbehaviour and how it was dealt with
- Keeping records of pupils' progress and success, or underachievement
- Pastoral review with senior manager to review group behaviour
- Writing references
- Contact with Special Educational Needs Co-Ordinator (SENCO) (re the Code of Practice)
- Contact with the educational psychologist, Education Welfare Officer, or other agencies
- Reading and signing reports
- Contacting parents either in writing or by telephone
- Induction arrangements, including placing pupils in pastoral groups
- Sending on records when pupils leave

- Keeping medical records up to date and ensuring other staff are aware of specific problems
- Parents' consultation evenings
- Contact with other social agencies
- Uniform checks
- Statistical returns, e.g. on the rate of authorised/unauthorised absence in the year group
- Pastoral staff induction and development
- Homework timetable
- Pupil planners

Personal organisation

Your personal organisation will play an important part in the way in which you manage and cope with your role. Effective personal organisation will be helped by:

1 Forward planning

It is important to have a clear overview of the sequence of the school year and to be aware of the demands of your particular pastoral group – for example, induction, option choices, transition arrangements. Year planners, such as the one in the Resource Bank at the back of this book (RB4), can help you and your pastoral team to plan for the 'hot spots' and keep track of events.

Year planner   RB4

Jan.	Feb.	March	April	May	June	July	Aug.	Sept.	Oct.	Nov.	Dec.

Using a daily personal planner can also help you feel more in control of the conflicting demands being made on your time. There are photocopiable versions of these personal planners in the Resource Bank at the end of the book.

Daily planner   RB5

Date:	
Before school	**Notes**
Break	**Notes**
Lunch	**Notes**
After school	**Notes**

Personal planner   RB6

Subject	Action to be taken	Deadline	Follow-up

2 Determining priorities

The kind of planning set out above can also help you with the task of determining your priorities. You will need to decide what is:

- urgent and requires immediate action
- important and needs to be done, but does not call for immediate action
- long term and needs some consideration
- information only and needs no further action
- unimportant.

These categories should have time-scales attached to them. Again, a planning form can help you to achieve effective planning.

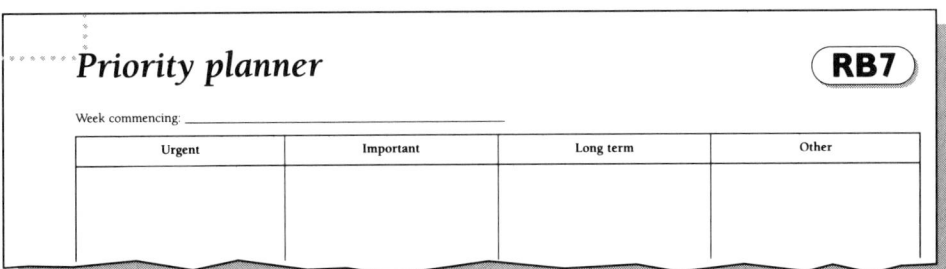

Priority planner   RB7

Week commencing: _____

Urgent	Important	Long term	Other

3 Good time management

Forward planning and prioritising help to produce effective time management. You should also consider:

- establishing routines; for example, setting aside time each week to clear paperwork, write letters, make telephone calls
- maintaining an orderly work place
- delegating responsibilities to others in your pastoral team

- referring routine clerical work to the school's administrative support team
- deciding which tasks should be done in school time and which cannot.

Your task as Pastoral Head is to see that the work is distributed equitably between the members of your team and that it is done efficiently. A good manager is one who uses time, resources and people effectively.

Communication

Effective communication relies upon seeing that the right people (staff, parents, governors and pupils) have all the information they need, at the appropriate time and in a form they can absorb. You need to consider:

- what you want to say
- how you want to say it (e.g. orally or in writing)
- who needs to know
- when they need to know.

Communication is most effective when it is:

- personal (i.e. one to one)
- straightforward, direct and fulfils a need or arouses interest
- presented clearly in an appropriate form
- conveyed at an appropriate time.

Written communication can be both an advantage and disadvantage in that:

- there is often a time difference between sending information and receiving a response (at times this can be useful)
- it can be retained as a record of communication
- the sender is able to review the information and his/her message in order to convey the information adequately
- it may convey your message more bluntly or forcefully than you intend.

Oral communication should be used as a starting point wherever possible, especially if there is something disturbing, threatening or urgent to communicate.

Meetings

Pastoral Heads normally meet regularly with their pastoral teams. Like all meetings held in school, these can have many different functions, but their value depends on how well they are planned and managed. Meetings are normally held to fulfil one or more of the following purposes:

- to determine, approve or promote policies
- to plan future developments and decide on a course of action
- to exchange information
- to monitor and evaluate aspects of the team's work.

To conduct effective meetings, you need to:

- allow enough time and plan in advance for important matters such as anti-bullying policy, behaviour management, monitoring of learners
- circulate agendas and discussion papers in advance
- appoint a colleague to record important decisions and action points and make these available to members of the senior management team
- deal with routine administrative matters by circular, mentioning them only briefly in the meeting
- give staff the opportunity to raise agenda items
- use meetings as in-service training sessions where appropriate, inviting members of the team, or others, to share expertise and new ideas
- invite the Headteacher or Pastoral Deputy or SENCO to attend when appropriate
- allocate some time for evaluation of work done – for example, use of resources
- celebrate success – for example, pupils' achievements.

Meetings should deal with matters of educational importance and colleagues should feel that time is well spent. Sheet RB8, in the Resource Bank, provides a checklist for running an effective meeting.

Working with tutors

Tutors form the 'inner circle' of the pastoral system and it is important for the Pastoral Head to have a clear understanding of their role. One school's attempt to identify the role and signal its importance is shown below.

FORM TUTORS

The duties of a form tutor include:

- keeping an accurate attendance register. This requires form tutors to be in their rooms promptly for registration
- collecting absence notes and completing the Optical Mark Reader (OMR) absence sheet as appropriate
- informing School Information Management System (SIMS) of any change in student details (e.g. address, telephone number)
- organising the work done in form assembly time according to the Year Head's guidelines
- escorting and supervising his/her form to, from and during Assembly
- creating a good *esprit de corps* in the form
- National Record of Achievement (NRA) profiling where appropriate
- contributing to and supervising the completion of school reports until handed to the year staff
- monitoring the wearing of school uniform
- issuing and making periodic checks of homework diaries
- monitoring any form tutor duties of associate teachers on teaching practice
- being part of the first line in the school's strategy for monitoring pupil welfare and dealing with discipline.

A sample job description for a form tutor is set out below and is included in the Resource Bank (RB9).

Sample job description  **RB9**

POST: Form tutor

The form tutor plays a very important role in the school, aiming to establish close relationships with the pupils in his/her care and getting to know them as individuals.

Together with the Head of Year the tutor takes an active lead in building the link between home and school, consulting with parents as the need arises.

The form tutor's responsibilities include:

1 Monitoring pupils' attendance

■ Contacting home when absences are unexplained after a period of two days.

■ Ensuring the prompt receipt of letters from parents explaining absence.

■ Sending out the standardised request for an explanation if not forthcoming.

■ Alerting the Head of Year to any problems or concerns regarding attendance.

2 Monitoring standards of appearance

■ Ensuring that the correct items of uniform are worn.

■ Ensuring that jewellery, make-up, etc. is not being worn.

3 Monitoring standards of behaviour

Helping to ensure that standards of behaviour are upheld by encouraging pupils to follow the School Code.

4 Homework

Checking homework journals regularly to ensure that these are kept up to date and signed by parents.

5 Disseminating information

Ensuring that published communications from school to home are effectively distributed and returns collected as necessary.

6 The PSHE Programme

Although the Head of Year provides the structure for the PSHE Programme, it is the tutor who plays the major role in interpreting and delivering the programme. Tutor evaluation of the programme is most valuable as part of the review process.

7 Profiling and reporting procedure

The tutor's role in profiling is an essential and demanding one in terms of organisation and implementation of the procedure. The tutor's skills in counselling and interviewing are integral to the profiling procedure. Increasingly, the profiling process will become an established part of the PSHE Programme. Good communication between the tutor, subject teachers, Head of Year and Senior Management is essential in order to ensure that any individual problems are resolved as effectively as possible.

8 Assemblies and reflection time

The tutor is responsible for ensuring that students move promptly and silently to assembly on the appropriate days. The tutor is also responsible for drawing up a schedule for the form to plan its reflection time in line with the guidelines.

In a large school, particularly, it is essential that provision is made for each student to be known as an individual. This is the fundamental role of the form tutor. Every tutor must concern him/herself with every student in the form if the school is not to become an impersonal organisation. Tutors are a vital link in the communications chain involving students, staff, parents, etc. Care and concern for the students extends to their personal appearance, attendance, punctuality and record of progress and achievements. The tutor should aim to achieve a professional relationship with each student, which enables difficulties to be sorted out before they become serious and which enables students to feel that they have someone to whom they can turn for help should problems arise.

The wider pastoral team

Pastoral teams in secondary schools involve, and interact with, a wider range of people, some of whom are regular visitors to the school. Make sure you get to know them and keep them involved with, and informed about, your pastoral group.

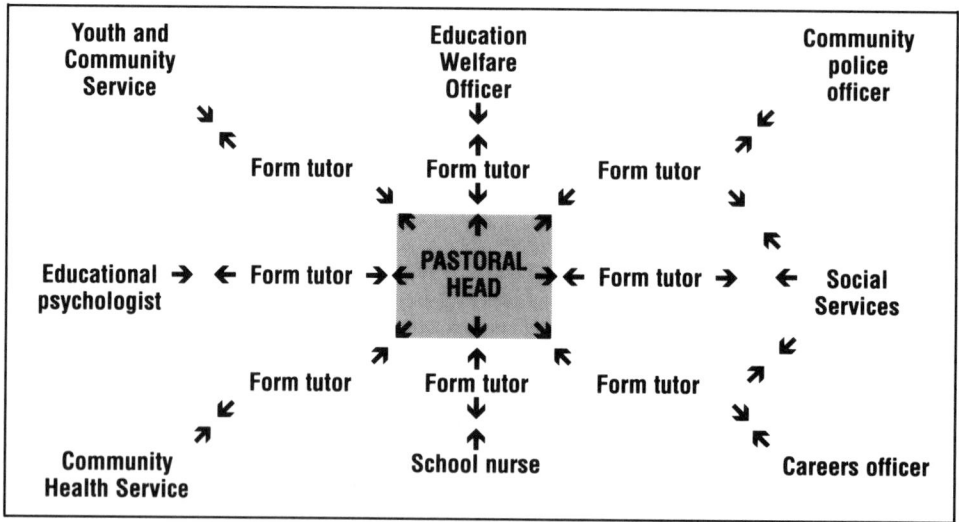

Make time in your tutorial/PSHE programme to introduce these people to your pastoral group and make sure that everyone in your tutor team is aware of the names, roles and functions of each of these people. The following is a brief guide:

Agency	Role and function
Education Welfare Officers (EWO)	Their main function is to follow up poor attendance, usually following a referral from the school. EWOs are trained in communication with families, counselling and problem solving and will try to use these skills to resolve attendance problems before resorting to prosecution. EWOs may also have some involvement in behavioural problems, exclusions, child protection and applications for family financial assistance.
Careers officers	Careers officers are regular visitors to secondary schools and are required to provide pupils with independent and accurate careers advice. They are likely to be involved in group and individual interviews with pupils in Years 9–13. A pupil who has an individual interview is provided with an Individual Action Plan.
School nurses	School nurses are part of the local community health scheme. Apart from being involved in health checks they may offer a confidential advice service for pupils. As this is likely to deal with issues such as contraception and drugs, the Pastoral Head needs to be well aware of school policy in this area.
Educational psychologists	They normally provide a locally agreed number of hours of involvement to each school. Inevitably, much of this time is taken up with assessments relating to the Code of Practice. Since their time is limited, you should prepare carefully for any involvement of the educational psychologist, paying particular attention to preparing detailed records of any pupils you wish to refer.

3 Pupil support and guidance

Induction

The successful Pastoral Head builds a relationship with all pupils for whom he/she is responsible and this begins with the induction process. Some schools favour a Head of Induction Year as a bridge between the contributory schools and the new school. This may be particularly appropriate when there are large numbers of contributory schools, social problems or children with special needs. The Head of Induction Year can build up more knowledge and experience than a Head of Year for whom the induction of a new cohort occurs only once every three, four or five years. Time spent planning the induction process is an investment in successful pastoral care which repays your efforts many times over.

The induction process should include:

- visits by the Pastoral Head to contributory schools whilst pupils are in their last year there
- opportunities for the Pastoral Head to become familiar to the year group (e.g. assemblies, concerts, plays, sports days, parents' evenings, etc.)
- arrangements for the transfer of records, both pastoral and academic, which should, wherever feasible, be in a common format agreed by all contributory schools. Make sure your department colleagues are aware of all the available information

and that they use it when drawing up set lists, etc. Failure to do this is still too common. It impedes children's progression and is a waste of the efforts of other professionals

- an induction day, or morning, for the year group at their new school. This day must be given high priority by all staff and needs to be planned with care
- an evening for 'new' parents at which they have the opportunity to meet the Pastoral Head and the member of the pastoral team who will be tutor to their child. This evening should be held late in the summer term before the children start at their new school, ideally a day or two after the pupils' induction day
- a parents' evening, with the Pastoral Head and tutors, eight to ten weeks after the pupils start at their new school and after an interim or 'settling in' report has been sent to parents.

A checklist like the one below will help you with your planning. A copy of this checklist is included in the Resource Bank (RB10).

Induction planning checklist   (RB10)

1	Have you made a preliminary visit to all the feeder schools?	Yes ☐	No ☐
2	Have you made arrangements for the transfer of academic information?	Yes ☐	No ☐
3	Have you agreed a common format for the transfer of academic information?	Yes ☐	No ☐
4	Have you made arrangements for the transfer of personal, medical or sensitive information?	Yes ☐	No ☐
5	Have you considered how this information will be transmitted to other staff?	Yes ☐	No ☐
6	Have you made arrangements for all important information about pupils' prior attainment and personal circumstances to be passed on to subject teachers?	Yes ☐	No ☐
7	Have you planned an induction day or session for new pupils?	Yes ☐	No ☐
8	Do all staff, including non-teaching staff, know what your plans are for the induction day?	Yes ☐	No ☐
9	Have you planned an evening for parents to meet their child's new tutor?	Yes ☐	No ☐
10	Have you planned a follow-up evening for parents early in the Autumn Term to follow up any initial concerns?	Yes ☐	No ☐

'The fresh start'

Whilst it is admirable that all children (and especially those with a less than perfect record) should feel they will have a completely fresh start at their new schools, it is unprofessional, foolish and potentially disastrous to take on a pastoral role without the benefit of as much background information as you can get.

Providing information for staff

The judgement of the Pastoral Head may be to keep certain information or details confidential, but medical and most background information should be given to all staff teaching those children. This is most effectively done at a meeting at the start of the year. Confidentiality is best protected if teachers make their own brief notes in their mark book after verbal explanation by the Pastoral Head, rather than by duplicating lists which are easily lost or seen by those for whom they are not intended.

Induction day

The importance of this day cannot be over-emphasised. It must be planned meticulously and *everyone* has a part to play. Even staff who do not have direct involvement should be fully informed and aware that they nevertheless have responsibilities. The exact format adopted is not important but it is vital to do everything possible to ensure that the new pupils have a positive experience of the school, which will allay their fears through the long summer holiday. A day in which the child meets a friendly and sympathetic tutor, enjoys a range of sample lessons, makes several new friends but then feels threatened by older pupils (even if they are joking) is not a good induction day and all your hard work and planning will have been wasted.

When planning the induction day:

- consult colleagues at the contributory schools early in the process. They will know far better than you which aspects of your school will excite your new charges and which will concern them
- timing is crucial. Make sure you have allowed enough time for activities and that everyone sticks to starting and finishing times. You should consider timings which differ from the normal school day your present pupils will be following (see the example in the box below). Remember when children are younger, nervous and

unfamiliar with the system, they are likely to take much longer than the norm to do such things as choosing and eating lunch

- new pupils are invariably the subject of great curiosity. Tell current pupils what is planned. Remind them how they felt at this time. Ask them to stay away from the induction year group; to organise some involvement of representative current pupils is a good idea but other than that it is better to keep the two groups apart if you can. Ask current pupils to show maturity by being helpful to any induction pupils they do meet

- it may be possible to take over parts of the school for the day to minimise the risk of unplanned meetings with older pupils and give the induction group a sense of ownership

- give the pupils something to take home. It confirms the impression that your school is well-organised, promotes discussion of the day between the pupils and their parents and generally helps to reinforce the idea of the induction day as a positive experience (see below)

- gather feedback from all possible sources – the children on the day, their teachers the following day, their parents at the 'new parents' meeting. Hopefully, all your feedback will be positive but even where it isn't, prompt action can turn a negative into a positive!

EXAMPLE: YEAR 9 INDUCTION MORNING

9.15 a.m.	Middle School pupils arrive
9.30 a.m.	ASSEMBLE – SMALL HALL (new tutors present) Address by Head and Head of Year 9 Introduction of new tutors Outline of first morning procedures
9.50 a.m.	Dismiss – to tutor bases with form tutors Introductions and handout of welcome folder Tutors accompany pupils to sample lessons
10.10 a.m.	Sample English lesson Sample Science lesson English/Science staff accompany pupils to SMALL HALL for break

11.05 a.m.	Break in SMALL HALL
	Orange juice and biscuits
	Informal exchange with selected Year 9 pupils
11.20 a.m.	English/Science staff collect pupils from SMALL HALL
	Sample English lesson
	Sample Science lesson
12.10 p.m.	English/Science staff accompany pupils to LARGE HALL for lunch
12.15 – 12.35 p.m.	Lunch in LARGE HALL
12.35 p.m.	Pupils return to Middle Schools

Induction pack

An induction pack, containing the basic information needed by new pupils joining the school, can be very helpful in making them feel welcomed and also in clarifying matters for parents. Typical contents of an induction pack are:

- a copy of the school's latest newsletter
- a welcome letter – e.g. from one or more of the following: the Headteacher, the Pastoral Head, the tutor, current pupils
- details of the school uniform – e.g. essential items, recommendations, games kit, requirements of other specific curriculum areas, rules regarding the wearing of jewellery, details of local suppliers
- information about organisational matters – e.g. details of tutor groups and registration procedures, movement around the school, conduct in lessons, school work (layout and presentation), homework, the school environment, bullying
- details of the extra-curricular activities – giving days, times, locations and sources of information
- a note about catering arrangements – e.g. a menu and tariff
- a plan of the school
- a key ring or pen.

Induction of pupils joining during the course of the school year

Moving schools is rarely easy for a child and tends to be particularly difficult for a teenager. For the younger child, the relationship with parents is often the mainstay, whereas the teenager may perceive friendships with peers to be the most important factor in life. The younger child's more open outlook means new friends are quickly made, the teenager may suffer from shyness or embarrassment as well as finding friendship groupings more firmly established and harder to join. Like the parent, the Pastoral Head can do little to influence the formation of friendships other than create the conditions for success by placing newcomers into groups where they are most likely to settle. In such situations, the well-being of the child is the important factor and if that means some tutor groups become slightly larger than others, then so be it!

When admitting a new pupil:

- wherever possible, arrange a visit with parent(s) to your school. Take as many details as possible. Observe the relationship between parent and child and how the child engages with you. He/she may well be nervous or worried, which could come over as surliness or brashness. You may find a totally different child once the parents have departed!
- take a walk around the school. This helps newcomers internalise the major change they face. It also begins the process of being seen by other pupils. Some schools arrange for newcomers to be taken around by existing pupils whilst the Pastoral Head talks to the parents. With the right mix of pupils, this can work well, but don't expect your image of the school to emerge totally unscathed from such encounters. The wrong guide can put the new pupil off the school and/or make acceptance more difficult by prejudicing classmates before the newcomer even starts at the school
- it quite often happens that the newcomer's first choice of friends is not the one the Pastoral Head would have hoped for. Such individuals or groups are usually easier to join and may be perceived by the newcomer initially as the only ones available. Like

the parent, the Pastoral Head may do more harm than good by interfering. Eventually, like will attract like and, in most cases, all will be well

- obtain all possible documentation from the pupil's previous school. Also, wherever possible, speak to the Pastoral Head or tutor responsible for the child (rather than the Headteacher or Deputy Head who are less likely to have detailed knowledge)

- consider very carefully the tutor group into which the new arrival will be placed. You may have a particularly sympathetic tutor, a group with an apparently similar disposition, or another recent arrival who has not yet had time to make firm friendships. Choosing the right tutor group is crucial to a good beginning and will be very important to the child. Although lessons occupy a much greater proportion of the total time spent in school, they are much more structured and directly controlled (one hopes!) by an adult. It is the time spent in registration and tutor periods which causes most anxiety to the newcomer

- insist that Head of Department colleagues make a full assessment of the new child's ability by studying the information available from the previous school and setting tests, if necessary. The 'we'll start him off in the middle set and see how he progresses' approach is unprofessional and unacceptable. The pressure to conform to a perceived norm is particularly strong in the newcomer to any organisation

- choose carefully the day the child will start with you. No one likes to be kept sitting around in an unfamiliar environment, so make sure you and your colleagues will be ready by the appointed day. Choose a day when you have non-contact time to help with the introductions or possible problems. The child will have to overcome disruption to his/her education anyway – a day or two spent unpacking in a new home or shopping for the school uniform is not going to make a significant difference. Where practicable, starting two or three days before a school holiday is ideal. The child is encouraged by the prospect of a break after the initial most difficult days, whilst for other pupils the newcomer is no longer a novelty by the start of the new term

- assure the child you will be following his/her progress in the first few weeks and will want to hear of any problems, however minor.

Be sure to repeat this to the parents as, sadly, the child will probably not believe you and will, anyway, feel inhibited in a new and unfamiliar environment

- observe the new pupil carefully in the first days and weeks and get others to do the same. Children will often tell you what they think you or their parents want to hear. Observation is more reliable. Unhappy children look unhappy and when children are frequently observed apart from their peers it usually means they are being rejected by them
- if you have concerns, arrange to see the child in your office or some other place which offers security and privacy, so that the child may feel confident talking about any problems.

Monitoring attendance and lateness

Monitoring attendance

The Pastoral Head needs to monitor attendance at several levels. Statistics must be used with care but the collection of statistical information is important and no useful judgements can be formed without such information. Where attendance is a general problem in the pastoral group, try to work closely with the Education Welfare Officer (EWO) to develop strategies such as:

- making use of an 'attendance report' to monitor particular pupils
- using assemblies to draw attention to the importance of good attendance and by awarding certificates for a 100% record or for improved attendance
- monitoring attendance figures closely and inviting the parents of pupils with unsatisfactory attendance rates or patterns to discuss the reasons for this
- involving the EWO and the community police officer in regular attendance checks, with follow-up visits to the homes of non-attenders

- communicating the school's attendance procedures clearly to parents (e.g. in an attendance leaflet) and stressing the importance of regular attendance
- setting up a 'one day absence' check with an immediate phone call home when a pupil suspected of truancy is absent.

Monitoring the year or house group

At a most basic level, attendance figures can be compared with national and local averages, between one cohort and another, and for the same cohort over different periods of time. The data is a useful starting point for questions, such as:

- *Why is the current Year 10's attendance worse than the previous three Year 10 groups?*

and for forming judgements:

- *Although the attendance of Year 11 in this school is slightly below the national average, it has improved significantly over the last three years.*

Monitoring the form or tutor group

If monitoring tutor groups highlights one with a significantly lower attendance level than the rest, this will certainly prompt a closer look. It may be simply explained by the presence in the group of one or two totally above-board long-term absentees. It may simply reflect a tutor's misinterpretation of the registration guidelines, but it may indicate a problem with tutors, pupils, or both, which needs attention.

Monitoring the individual

The Pastoral Head must ensure that tutors understand and follow clear guidelines on registration and attendance, so that patterns and discrepancies quickly become apparent. Five separate one-day absences are much more significant than a week's absence, which probably indicates a bout of flu or something similar. It is even more interesting if those five days were all on the same day of the week! Casual enquiries to peers may well elicit some useful information to be followed up. Letting the pupil know that you are concerned about the pattern of absence will sometimes be enough in itself to improve matters. If not, the next stage is to take the matter up with the parents. Again, this may be enough in itself. Perhaps the parents will stop keeping the pupils off school as the most convenient way to look after a younger child. However, perhaps this will just be the opening shot in a long campaign!

Monitoring lateness

As with attendance, it is the role of the Pastoral Head to monitor punctuality to school and take action if improvement is needed. Similar procedures should be initiated to monitor and improve lateness as are used for absence. Lateness to school, like absenteeism, is a symptom that all is not well.

The first requirement is to have clear guidelines which *all* tutors follow. Teachers hold very different perceptions of punctuality (including, sometimes, a very relaxed view of their own!). You cannot collect meaningful information unless there is common agreement on what is meant by lateness, as well as consistency in recording and dealing with it. Once you have a system in place you can monitor punctuality in much the same ways as attendance, imposing the overall standard and concentrating your fire on the hard core of offenders.

'The late book'

Most school offices maintain a late book, but whether this is a work of fiction or a useful record depends on the attitude of all concerned – in particular the Pastoral Head, who should check the book on at least a weekly basis. The record will include those pupils arriving late after legitimate appointments with hospitals, dentists, etc. Ensure, though, that there is a procedure for following through on such appointments. There will be those who appear on odd occasions in the book because they have overslept, missed the school bus or something similar. The most important thing is that the late book is checked regularly by Pastoral Heads and followed up where reasons for lateness are unsatisfactory. For these pupils, the mere knowledge that their lateness has been recorded and will come to the attention of their tutor and Head of Year, will be sufficient deterrent.

The persistent latecomer

Many schools have a core of persistent latecomers, who often show ingenuity and creativity in completing the 'reason for lateness' section. In a minority of cases they may be late through no fault of their own – perhaps travelling to school by car with a disorganised or unco-operative parent. In most cases, there is no real excuse and the Pastoral Head must show persistence and ingenuity in tackling the cause – for instance, telephoning the house of a child who goes back to sleep after being roused by a parent who then goes out to work. Remember that pressure on late arrivals may cause them to stop signing the late book whilst still arriving late. Vigilant subject teachers and tutors should detect this and the even more serious situation where the child takes the day off rather than coming to school late.

Ten further ways to improve attendance and punctuality – a checklist   (RB11)

1 Have you checked your guidelines? You may be recording as absence something which other schools count as attendance (e.g. work experience, fieldwork, etc.).	Yes ☐	No ☐
2 Have you stressed the importance of good attendance and punctuality through assemblies? (Remember not to nag though – it can be counter-productive!)	Yes ☐	No ☐
3 Have you sent parents a clear explanation of the importance of good attendance, and what you are doing to improve attendance rates?	Yes ☐	No ☐
4 Have you made it clear to pupils and parents that medical and dental appointments should not be in school time? Do you insist that if such appointments are unavoidable, the pupil attends before/after the appointment?	Yes ☐	No ☐
5 Do you ensure that form tutors receive an explanation for all absence and late arrival and do you occasionally take a random sample of pupils to follow up their reasons for yourself? (Remember to use the Education Welfare Officer to follow up the more persistent problems, and be prepared to challenge and disbelieve parents on occasions. You may not be popular but you will secure improvement.)	Yes ☐	No ☐
6 Have you set up incentive schemes such as rewards, letters home or certificates for good attendance or punctuality? (These can have a significant effect, especially when built up over time.)	Yes ☐	No ☐
7 Have you considered the example set by colleagues? Are there certain issues which senior management should be raising with certain individuals either about their own attendance and punctuality, or about condoning the absence of some of the more difficult pupils?	Yes ☐	No ☐
8 Are you aware of any pupils working illegally or just working long hours to the detriment of their education and attendance?	Yes ☐	No ☐
9 Are you aware of using employers constructively to stress the importance of good attendance and punctuality?	Yes ☐	No ☐
10 Is the work ethic of the school a positive one, or do lessons start late or finish early; does little work happen on the last day of term, etc.?	Yes ☐	No ☐

Lateness check

It is an interesting and instructive exercise for a team of Pastoral Heads and senior management to station one or more of their number at every one of the school's entrances and note the numbers arriving after the bell and their time of arrival. Not only does this give an interesting overall picture, it can also turn out to be a comment on how promptly certain tutors get to registration!

Behaviour – dealing with incidents

As Pastoral Head you will frequently be called upon to deal with incidents, usually at the most inconvenient or busy time. Whatever the pressures, consistency and fairness must always be the aim. This includes consideration for those pupils taught by you. You should leave your classroom only for the most serious and urgent reasons. Nearly all incidents, including the most serious, can be dealt with, or at least contained, by others until you are free to deal with it. This is especially so if there are clear guidelines on procedures for staff (see Chapter 4).

When dealing with these kinds of incidents:

- be calm and decisive over your initial arrangements. Others around you (staff included) may be highly charged and try to pressure you into arriving at judgements and taking action which you are not yet ready to do
- where pupils have become very upset or angry, give them space to recover (under unobtrusive supervision) before talking to them
- don't let the main protagonists re-run the incident in front of you, even if one is a colleague. The atmosphere will become more tense, the positions more entrenched. Tactfully separate them and arrange to hear both sides of the dispute and any witnesses as soon as you can
- make your own notes when you interview those involved (see 'Interviewing witnesses', below) though also ensure they write a

statement of their own either before or after your interview (see the incident report form, RB12, in the Resource Bank at the end of this book)

- when dealing with a group of pupils suspected of wrongdoing, keep them separate. Start your enquiries with those least likely to be the main culprits. This will increase the psychological pressure on the ringleaders and enable you to build up an accurate picture of the incident with which to confront them

- don't let the children suspected of serious wrongdoing back into lessons until your inquiry is complete and you have dealt with the misbehaviour (or at least reached an interim decision, perhaps to refer the incident to a higher authority). This gives a clear message that the school regards the incident as serious and prevents the pupils from enjoying notoriety or intimidating witnesses.

You will rarely have the luxury of dealing completely with any incident before the intervention of another lesson, parental interview or the end of the school day. This is unfortunate but unavoidable. A number of strategies exist which can be helpful when your work on the incident has to start and stop several times. It is often possible to 'make a virtue out of necessity' and use an enforced delay to good effect in resolving a problem. Pupils waiting whilst you teach a lesson or interview others should use the time to write a full account of the incident. This time to calm down and reflect on his/her actions is often sufficient in itself to bring about remorse and a willingness to apologise and make amends.

Interviewing witnesses

When investigating an incident, interview witnesses one by one. Warn them that if you later find out something they did not tell you, it will cast doubt on everything they *did* say. Listen carefully to each account, making detailed notes on a separate sheet. Establish where they were, what they saw, what they heard, said and did. Compare the accounts you have taken. Work to eliminate or explain any discrepancies, if necessary by seeing pupils again. Gradually you will form a picture of what took place.

When conducting such interviews:

- *insist that you will find the truth* – explain that what is done cannot be undone but the sooner the truth is established the sooner the matter can be dealt with so that everyone can move forward

- *always respect a confidence* – if four or five people are interviewed no one need ever know where your information came from. You do not have to tell the parents of offenders the source of your information as long as you are sure it is correct·

- *keep witnesses apart* – especially those you suspect of wrongdoing. This is still important even if they have had some time together

- *don't be rushed into action* before you are satisfied you know exactly what happened and each pupil's part in it

- *remember that the truth is in the detail* – experienced miscreants stick as closely as possible to the truth but make their own part seem innocuous and alter the sequence of events to conceal their responsibility as instigator

- *insist on language that has clear meaning* – thus, 'I was just messing about with him. He gave me some verbal so I had a go at him', should probably be translated as, 'I was verbally and/or physically bullying a weaker pupil. Eventually he was provoked into calling me a name. I then punched him several times.'

Interviewing pupils who are worried or upset

When arranging to interview such pupils, consider first that they may prefer to talk to someone other than you – perhaps a favourite teacher or a teacher of the same sex. It might help to allow the pupil to have a friend present, for moral support. Seat pupils comfortably, ideally at the same level as yourself, with a physical barrier such as a coffee table between you. Don't hurry them. Talk quietly and be reassuring. Begin with open questions and keep them brief. Explain that there are some matters you are not allowed to keep confidential if you are told about them, but you will always give your support. Document the interview but use your discretion as to how and when this is best done.

Contact with parents

Many parents, particularly of children who cause difficulties at school, have unhappy memories of their own schooldays. They feel defensive and may be reluctant to come into school for an interview with someone better educated and more articulate. Pastoral Heads should be aware that most parents want their children to do well at school and can be brought into partnership with the right approach.

Unfortunately, there are no shortcuts. Good communication requires considerable investment of time. The earlier this begins the better. It may prevent the onset of more serious misbehaviour, but even if it doesn't it will lay the foundation of a relationship with parents which will hold up when things become more difficult.

Sometimes, young people exhibit anti-social behaviour in school which is not seen in the home. It may then be difficult to persuade parents that there is a problem. Be patient but persistent. If a child is behaving unacceptably at school it is the duty of the parents to co-operate with you. Misbehaviour at school often foreshadows difficult behaviour at home. Many Pastoral Heads have dealt with parents who initially dismissed school concerns as groundless only to admit within a few months that they had lost control of their child!

Communication by letter

A busy Pastoral Head will need to write many letters during a school year and needs the support and understanding of the school's administrative staff as well as a sound filing system.

Communicating by letter has several advantages:

- letters are relatively quick and convenient
- they can be drafted and re-drafted until the right balance is achieved
- they allow you to describe the problem as you see it, without interruption
- parents cannot later deny knowledge of the contents of a letter, especially if you include a reply slip asking them to acknowledge receipt

- parents can read a letter several times over, which may help them to understand the points you wish to communicate.

But:

- letters may be intercepted or explained away by the pupil
- parents may feel alienated by the formality of a typewritten letter on school headed notepaper
- letters can be ignored or forgotten by even the best-intentioned parents.

When writing to parents:

- keep the language you use simple and straightforward
- keep sentences short and uncomplicated
- try to avoid sounding too formal and unfriendly
- make it clear what the problems are, how they relate to the school's rules or expectations and how matters can be put right
- refer to earlier problems, warnings, letters, telephone conversations or meetings.

Use a letter for minor transgressions (or praise!) or to document serious problems or warnings, ideally in combination with a telephone conversation or meeting. Letters alone, especially a series detailing negative behaviour with no attempt to engage parents on a more personal level, are very unlikely to achieve the desired outcome.

Telephoning parents

The telephone allows the Pastoral Head to enter into a proper dialogue with parents who may be more relaxed and open to discussion in the comfort and security of their own home. Be prepared for the conversation to take longer than you had expected. Be careful of the unguarded comment or the statement that is capable of misinterpretation – whether accidental or deliberate!

When telephoning parents:

- before you dial, make brief notes of the points you wish to make. Where you expect conversation to be difficult, list certain sentences or phrases you want to be sure to have said. These notes, together with a brief comment written after the call, can also serve as a record of what was said

- say at the outset who you are and why you are telephoning. Parents frequently forget names, fail to understand school hierarchies or transition arrangements
- refer briefly to earlier conversations or meetings, especially where there has been a positive outcome
- be patient and explain clearly. You are familiar with the problem, you know the part their child played, you know the school rules. Parents take some time to understand what happened and why the school regards the problem as serious
- be firm, don't be drawn into an argument or be diverted by other matters. Offer a face-to-face meeting if it seems appropriate but point out you are telephoning in an attempt to save the parents' time and the inconvenience of a meeting in school.

Meeting parents to discuss problems

Always time-consuming and sometimes stress-inducing, a face-to-face meeting with parents is often the best way to resolve a problem. Make sure you have allowed sufficient time for the interview to run its course. Ensure the meeting takes place in a comfortable and private location (if this is your office, take the telephone off the hook and get a 'Do not disturb' sign for the door). After-school meetings may inconvenience you but working parents will appreciate your consideration of their difficulties and you will find you can concentrate better when the day's other distractions are behind you.

As always, preparation is the key to a successful outcome. Make a brief list of points you wish to cover (you may wish to give parents a copy and work through it with them).

When interviewing parents:

- be positive – emphasise your desire for co-operation and a partnership of equals in the best interests of the child
- be straightforward – avoid jargon, keep it simple without patronising the parent
- be clear about the facts – the parent will have heard the child's version but not the school's

- let parents have their say – don't monopolise the discussion. Acknowledge failings on the part of the school if such comments are fair – this will help you achieve your main objectives
- try to establish a consensus – summarise areas of agreement before the interview ends.

It may be helpful to bring the child into the interview after any confidential matters have been discussed and when broad agreement has been reached. At this point the child will see the Pastoral Head and parent acting together. The situation in which the child is an interested onlooker of a heated argument between parent and Pastoral Head should be avoided at all costs!

Seeing parents in their home

Such meetings may arise spontaneously when the child has had to be taken home because of illness or a problem at school. You are most likely to arrange a home visit when parents have difficulty (or make excuses) about coming into school. It is likely to give you a deeper understanding of the background to a child's problems. It may be very much appreciated by parents who see it as evidence of your good faith and desire to support them. Nevertheless, such visits can be unpredictable and are not for the inexperienced.

Before visiting parents at home:

- ensure that both parents know you will be visiting, what you want to talk about and how long you expect the visit to last
- explain that, because the matter is important and you want to consider carefully the points they have to make, you must all be able to talk without distraction
- ensure that the child whose problems you wish to discuss knows what to expect and will not suddenly deny at home things admitted in school. The child can also be helpful in reinforcing with the parents the need for suitable conditions in which to talk
- be prepared to change your role. Though you may have acted as prosecutor in school and at the beginning of the interview, you may need to plead for the defence subsequently if the parents' response to the child's behaviour is too severe

- remember that parents will not have full knowledge of the problem being discussed or of the school rules and expectations. They may have been given a less than comprehensive account by the child in question. Take your time and be prepared to explain several times over. Be sympathetic, not confrontational, to the natural desire of most parents to defend their own child
- be prepared for diversionary tactics. Some parents will suddenly raise matters that have no relevance to the situation under discussion (e.g. 'How come he never gets any homework?'). See if you can spot any issues by asking the child before you go. If other matters are raised, calmly explain that you will take note and investigate but that you must first finish the discussion you came for.

It is a good idea to take a colleague with you, especially when you have not visited before or have reason to anticipate difficulty. As with other meetings, follow up your visit with a letter, thanking the parents for seeing you and setting out briefly but clearly what was discussed and agreed.

Bullying

Bullying has been described as a systematic and persistent attempt by an individual or a group to impose his/her/their will on another. This action can involve violence, threats, verbal assaults or deliberate isolation. It is a topic of concern to pupils, parents and teachers, and a great deal of research has recently been carried out into proactive approaches for detecting and countering bullying. Good advice is available from organisations such as Kidscape on how to manage bullying and many schools will have developed and in some cases, published, whole-school approaches on the issue.

Whatever system your school employs, as Pastoral Heads you will need to:

- be vigilant – bullies are often very adept at covering their tracks
- take reported incidents seriously and investigate them thoroughly
- ensure that subject staff and form tutors monitor any incident of bullying, using a form like RB13 from the Resource Bank. One

incident can be part of a much more extensive pattern of bullying experienced by an individual pupil and it is important that all incidents are monitored and that the Pastoral Head has a thorough overview

■ ensure that you keep good records of any incidents of bullying you have dealt with. Provide a summary log to your line manager who will have senior management responsibility for ensuring that bullying is minimised and that if incidents do take place, they are followed up effectively. Form RB14 can be used for this purpose

■ follow up any pupil who has been bullied to ensure that there has been no continuation of the problem.

Bullying report form — (RB13)

Please fill in and pass this to the form tutor of any child involved in *any* incident of bullying. The form tutor will ensure that it is passed to the Pastoral Head.

NAME: _____ YEAR: _____

DATE: _____ TIME: _____

DETAILS OF INCIDENT:

ACTION TAKEN:

Signed:_____

Form tutor comment/action:

Pastoral Head comment/action:

Transition

These days, few of our pupils go straight into full-time, permanent employment if they choose to leave school at 16, yet many young people and their parents seem still to believe that 'something will turn up' miraculously towards the end of the summer term. It is never too early to begin preparations for the next phase. Good careers advice is essential. Target setting and the construction of pupil records of achievement can be extremely helpful in getting young people to appreciate their own potential and the opportunities open to them.

For the majority at 16, the choice will be some form of training placement, a Further Education college course, a place at tertiary or sixth-form college, or staying on at school. Pastoral Heads will be aware of a possible conflict of interest here and remember that their role is to guide pupils towards the choice most appropriate to their needs and *not* to ensure as many of the year group as possible return to the sixth form, regardless of their own interests or suitability!

The Pastoral Head is, by now, very knowledgeable about the pupils. But he/she cannot be expected to have detailed, up-to-date knowledge of the course options and course requirements of all routes open to pupils. The next stage is best handled by a team, of whom the Pastoral Head may be one. Ideally, every pupil concerned should be interviewed by one of the team and a proforma completed. This approach reinforces the status of the pupils as of equal importance whatever their level of ability. Where necessary, pupils are referred on to a careers officer, college of Further Education, heads of sixth form or teachers of particular sixth-form/advanced-level subjects. Assessing potential for A level courses is a vital task, as it leads on to important and expensive decisions about curriculum and staffing. It is not something the Pastoral Head should be expected to do. He/she is much more profitably employed advising the team on certain individuals, overseeing the process of recording achievement, writing confidential references, maintaining an up-to-date record of pupil destinations and supporting the unsuccessful and the undecided.

Behaviour management and the Code of Practice

Behaviour management

The idea of Pastoral Heads being involved in 'behaviour management' is a relatively new one and developed in the UK after the publication of the Elton Report. Of course, Pastoral Heads have always tried to manage or resolve the problem behaviour of individual pupils. However, in the past, they tended to act largely on their own or in the context of their own pastoral team, reacting to problems of behaviour rather than trying proactively to manage and improve all problematic pupil behaviour.

The publication of the Elton Report in 1989 encouraged schools to develop a more systematic approach to the monitoring and management of problem behaviour.

The Elton Report studied the kinds of behaviour that caused teachers (and pupils) most concern. Contrary to popular views, teachers were not found to be frequently dealing with incidents of violent misbehaviour. However, the report showed that the sort of behaviour that teachers found most difficult to deal with was lower level but, nevertheless, persistent misbehaviour. This included:

- talking out of turn
- hindering other pupils
- calculated idleness or work avoidance
- verbal abuse towards other pupils.

Elton suggested that schools should have whole-school behaviour policies so that this behaviour could be managed and improved through consistent action and the involvement of staff, pupils and parents. It also identified the kinds of 'discipline' which did not seem to work.

'. . . schools which simply have long lists of prohibitions and no consistent behaviour policy are more likely to be troubled by bad behaviour than those which have harmonised all the features of the institution concerned with behaviour.'

'. . . punitive regimes seem to be associated with worse rather than better standards of behaviour.'

(Elton Report, 1989)

Whole-school behaviour policies

Following the Elton Report, many schools developed whole-school behaviour policies. Such policies are effective when they:

- involve staff, pupils, parents and governors in developing a *shared* view of what kind of behaviour is unacceptable
- clearly identify a range of sanctions which can be applied *consistently*
- adopt a *staged* approach to sanctions so that the child who misbehaved understood the consequences of further misbehaviour
- involve good communication with the tutor and parents. *Parents are to be involved at an earlier stage* in any action to remedy misbehaviour

- involve the systematic *monitoring and recording* of pupils' behaviour and their response to any intervention to bring about improvement
- *clarify roles and responsibilities* within the school so that there is no confusion about when and how action was to be taken and by whom
- balance sanctions with a *policy of praise* and encouragement.

EXAMPLE OF CHECKLIST FOR USE WITH WHOLE-SCHOOL BEHAVIOUR POLICIES

Checklist for your school

Does your school have a whole-school behaviour policy?   Yes ☐ No ☐

Was this policy agreed by staff, pupils, parents and governors?   Yes ☐ No ☐

Have all parents had a copy of it?   Yes ☐ No ☐

Does the policy balance sanctions with rewards and praise?   Yes ☐ No ☐

Does it clarify different responsibilities for action?   Yes ☐ No ☐

Are sanctions staged (i.e. do they move from less serious to more serious in relation to either persistent low-level misbehaviour or serious misbehaviour)?   Yes ☐ No ☐

Does the policy link into the school's exclusions policy?   Yes ☐ No ☐

Does the policy link into the Code of Practice?   Yes ☐ No ☐

Are parents/significant adults involved and informed at an early stage?   Yes ☐ No ☐

If many of your answers to this checklist are negative, you may feel that your current school behaviour policy needs reviewing.

The Code of Practice

Before you and others review your school's behaviour policy, you should take account of an important further development which has had an impact on the way schools choose to manage problem behaviour. In some schools the Code of Practice for pupils with Special Educational Needs (SEN) (introduced in 1993) is operated as a separate system. However, as it also deals with pupils whose behaviour or emotional problems are having an impact on their learning, it is helpful to try to integrate it with your behaviour management system. This is also important because there may be an undiagnosed learning difficulty at the root of the behaviour that you are trying to deal with.

The impact of the Code of Practice on behaviour management

The Code of Practice for pupils with SEN identified a staged process which schools had to work through, which applied to pupils whose learning difficulties were caused by emotional or behavioural problems as well as those with language or other learning difficulties. At each stage, parents were to be involved, and the action taken was to be formalised in Special Arrangements or an Individual Education Plan. In the later stages, specialist support was to be sought, particularly from the school's educational psychologist.

The first requirement is for the Pastoral Head to become familiar with the system which the school's SENCO (Special Educational Needs Co-Ordinator) is operating. It is important for the Code of Practice to be integrated into the school's behaviour policy, and schools have to have internal systems which ensure that Pastoral Heads and SENCOs work closely together. Pastoral Heads may need training in working with the SENCO to devise Special Arrangements or write Individual Education/Behaviour Plans and it is even more important that pupil misbehaviour and attempts to modify it are carefully documented.

Example: Operation of the SEN Code of Practice

STAGE 1
- Initial identification of problem.
- Pupil's name placed on Register of Concern and Special Arrangements.
- Parent/s involved.
- Special Arrangements made and review date agreed.

❶

SPECIAL ARRANGEMENTS REPORT

Several reviews undertaken to gauge if problem behaviour has improved.

Review ⇩ Review

STAGE 2
- If there has been no improvement, the pupil will move to Stage 2.
- Involvement of SENCO and others in diagnostic work (e.g. analysis of literacy level, medical checks, etc. where appropriate).
- Parent/s involved.
- Individual Behaviour Plan made and review date agreed.

❷

INDIVIDUAL BEHAVIOUR PLAN REPORT

Review ⇩ Review

STAGE 3
- If there has been no improvement, the pupil will move to Stage 3.
- Further involvement of SENCO and outside agencies (e.g. advice from educational psychologist).
- Involvement of parent/s or 'significant adult'.
- More detailed Individual Behaviour Plan agreed involving 'contract' between school, parent/s and pupil, and modification to timetable if appropriate.

❸

CONTRACT REPORT

Review ⇩ Review

STAGE 4
- If there has been no improvement, move pupil to Stage 4.
- Involvement of educational psychologist in developing a specialist Behaviour Modification plan. This may involve some education/training off site.
- Involvement of parent/s.

❹

SPECIALIST BEHAVIOUR MODIFICATION PLAN

Review ⇩ Review

STAGE 5
- If there has been no improvement, the school may have to consider permanent exclusion. In theory, this could lead to the pupil gaining specialist education elsewhere. In practice this is often difficult to obtain.

- Special schools (e.g. EBD schools*) are unlikely to take pupils who have not first been formally excluded.

❺

EVIDENCE PRESENTED TO GOVERNORS

❻

INFORMATION SENT TO LEA

---

* Schools for pupils with Emotional and Behavioural Difficulties.

This example is from an 11–18 high school. Schools will interpret the application of the various Stages in ways that suit their own circumstances and will develop their own forms of monitoring pupil responses. In this example:

- behavioural problems are clearly identified by the Pastoral Head who has a fortnightly review meeting with a senior manager
- a decision is taken about the seriousness of the problem and whether the pupil's behaviour justifies placing him/her on the Code of Practice Register of Concern and Special Arrangements
- once it is agreed to place the pupil on this register, the SENCO needs to be informed, both so that the register is updated, and so that he/she can eventually be involved (e.g. in initial screening of reading ability, which may be a factor in the pupil's misbehaviour)
- the school uses a series of report formats which are used both to monitor pupil response and to inform all teaching staff of action to be taken.

A staged approach to managing behaviour

As the example above shows, the Code of Practice operates in stages with the parent/s being fully involved at every stage. Once a pupil is identified as causing concern he/she may be put onto the first stage.

It is important for you to try to work through the stages, reviewing progress as necessary. This is particularly important if you reach a point where you feel that the appropriate sanction is permanent exclusion, since you will have to demonstrate that you have exhausted all the possibilities within the school before taking the step of excluding the child from the school.

Generally there should be at least two reviews over a reasonable time scale before the pupil is moved to the next stage, and parents or 'significant adults' should be involved at every stage to ensure support and understanding of the process.

Stage 1

Operation of the code of practice	You will need:
Identification of pupil to move to Stage 1.	■ **a system for monitoring and recording incidents of misbehaviour (see RB15, Pupil referral form)** ■ **to keep a clear summary record of the pupil's behaviour and the strategies the school has used, before you consider putting the pupil on the Register of Concern and any Special Arrangements are established (see RB16)** ■ **a regular pastoral review to consider all pupils causing concern. A proforma such as RB17 will be helpful here. This pastoral review should involve the Pastoral Head and the senior manager responsible for pastoral care. It is suggested that reviews take place every 3–4 weeks and that a record of decisions is kept on a proforma (see RB17)** ■ **an agreed and consistent view of when behaviour is causing sufficient concern to trigger a move to Stage 1** ■ **an agreed view of strategies for modifying behaviour, which are appropriate for use at an initial stage. Usually this will involve monitoring the pupil's behaviour in lessons more closely** ■ **the involvement of the pupil's parent/s** ■ **to consider whether reference to the SENCO is appropriate at this stage.**

Examples of proformas referred to above are explained below, and are included in the Resource Bank at the back of this book.

PUPIL REFERRAL FORM

To be filled in by the classroom teacher and then passed onto form tutor and then the Pastoral Head.

Pupil:
Class: Date: Period:
Teacher:

Cause for concern (give precise details of incident/behaviour):

Action taken:

Form tutor comment/action:

Pastoral Head comment/action:

RETAIN ON FILE

A form like the pupil referral form shown above, gives the school a straightforward way of monitoring pupil behaviour. It is only filled in when the pupil reaches a certain stage and the expectation is that the classroom teacher will take initial action to deal with the behaviour (unless it is a serious incident which needs to be referred immediately). If a form tutor (and then the Pastoral Head) receive a number of referrals in a short space of time, they will know that the pupil has a more widespread behaviour difficulty, and action can be taken. A slightly different pupil referral form is included in the Resource Bank (RB15).

Behaviour monitoring form   RB16

Pupil:

Form: Year:

Date	Details of behavioural problem/incident	School response	Parents informed

A form like RB16 can be used when a pupil is being considered for Stage 1 of the Code of Practice. It provides evidence that the pupil's behaviour has been monitored and that the initial strategies for behaviour management have already been tried.

Pastoral review form   RB17

Year:		Head of Year:		Date:	
Pupil's name	Sex	Cause for concern	Agreed action		Review date

The pastoral review form (RB17) can act as a record of the Pastoral Head's review meeting with his/her line manager, and as a means of communication with the SENCO, where the agreed action is that the pupil is placed on one of the stages of the Code of Practice.

The following flow diagram summarises the process described above in which it is decided to move the pupil to Stage 1 of the Code of Practice.

EXAMPLE: STAGE 1 IN OPERATION

The school has a system of referral forms which a teacher fills in when a pupil misbehaves to the extent that they are breaking the school's Code of Behaviour.

The referrals are sent first to the form tutor to keep him/her informed and then to the Head of Year. The subject teacher is expected to take initial action unless the incident is a serious one.

When the Head of Year has 3 or 4 referrals for the same pupil in a short space of time, the pupil is considered at the monthly review meeting which the Pastoral Head has with the SENCO and the Deputy Head responsible for pastoral care. Information will also be sought from the form tutor. If there is general concern about the pupil's behaviour, he/she will be put onto Stage 1 for the Register of Concern and Special Arrangements.

The SENCO may be asked to test and assess the pupil to see if there are any language or learning problems of which the school is unaware, which may be contributing to the pupil's problem behaviour.

A range of possible strategies to improve the pupil's behaviour will be discussed. These could include:

- daily report for some/all subjects
- individual targets for improvement
- detention or loss of privileges if behaviour continues

- follow-up discussion with Head of subject if inappropriate teaching materials are contributing to the problem.

Following the advice of the Elton Report, the school believes that it is important to involve the parent/s at an early stage of any behavioural problem and no final decision is made about the Special Arrangements for the pupil until parents have been consulted and the action discussed with the pupil as well.

The Special Arrangements are agreed and conveyed to all teachers via the Special Arrangements Report (which the pupil takes to all lessons) so that consistent enforcement is possible. This allows the Pastoral Head to monitor the situation on a daily or weekly basis.

The pupil's behaviour is monitored and reviewed so that the pupil can be moved off the Register of Concern and Special Arrangements as soon as possible.

Once you have decided to move a pupil to Stage 1 you need to ensure that the school's SENCO is informed, and that the pupil's name goes onto the school's Register of Concern and Special Arrangements.

You will need to identify what Special Arrangements you are making for this pupil, and you will need to ensure that you provide all staff teaching the pupil with details of the Special Arrangements you are making for him/her.

Register of Concern and Special Arrangements (RB18)

			CODE OF PRACTICE SPECIAL ARRANGEMENTS/INDIVIDUAL EDUCATION PLANS					
Year:			Date of issue:					
Name	Form	Stage	Cause for concern	Arrangements/IEP	Review	Review	Review	Stage

You will also have to think about the way information is communicated to staff teaching the pupil. Confidentiality has to be balanced against the importance of all staff acting on the agreed Special Arrangements to ensure consistency and maximum reinforcement of the arrangements. The following is an example of Special Arrangements for a pupil whose behaviour is affecting his/her learning.

Special Arrangements Report (RB19)

Code of Practice Stage 1

Dear Parent/Guardian

It has been necessary to place your child on daily report to help improve his/her behaviour. Please check and sign the report every day. The report will also be checked daily by his/her form teacher.

Pastoral Head

Pupil: _____   Form: _____   Review date: _____

Please comment on the following: Behaviour/Attitude (additional comments can be made on reverse)

	Reg.	1	2	3	4	5	6	Staff signature	Parent's signature
Monday									
Tuesday									
Wednesday									
Thursday									
Friday									

This report should be completed and returned to _____ (Pastoral Head).

If problem behaviour occurs, please complete the section below.

Details of any problem behaviour (additional details can be given on reverse)

Date/lesson	What led up to the incident?	What happened?	What were the consequences?	Staff signature

The Special Arrangements Report has several functions. It:

- tells each subject teacher what the problem is
- tells each subject teacher what the arrangements are
- helps monitor whether Special Arrangements have been successfully carried out by staff and pupils
- collects evidence of the antecedents to any further problem behaviour, specifies accurately the nature of the problem behaviour and lists the consequences.

This information is particularly important if the pupil has to move to the next stage.

After several reviews, you may need to move to Stage 2.

Stage 2

Operation of the code of practice	You will need:
Pupil has not responded to the Special Arrangements and these have been reviewed several times.	■ a method of monitoring and evaluating pupil progress or lack of progress and of collecting detailed evidence about the problem behaviour, its antecedents and consequences. The Special Arrangements Report mentioned above will do this ■ an agreed view of when a pupil should be moved to Stage 2. This is important to ensure consistency between different year groups ■ more involvement from the SENCO (e.g. in testing the pupil's literacy, language and numeracy skills to see if poor behaviour is linked to frustration with performance in these areas) ■ access to advice from specialists (e.g. educational psychologist, EWO). However, the educational psychologist is not normally involved in interviewing an individual pupil until Stage 3/4. Schools will need to make their own decisions here depending on the availability of educational psychologist hours ■ involvement of more senior colleagues (e.g. Headteacher/Deputy Head) ■ more detailed involvement of parent/s or the 'significant adult' in the child's life ■ to provide an Individual Behaviour Plan (IBP) for this pupil. Again it can be in the form of a report which the pupil takes to his/her teachers. At this stage, the problem behaviour needs to be clearly broken down into defined behaviour/s which the pupil and the school will agree to work on.

Individual Behaviour Plan and Report (RB20)

Code of Practice Stage 2

One form for each day of the school week

Dear Parent/Guardian

Your child has been placed on an individual behaviour plan/report to improve his/her behaviour. Please check and sign the report every day. The report will also be checked daily by the Pastoral Head.

Name of student: _____

Tutor group: _____ Date: _____

Note: Would staff please tick if these targets have been met or put a cross if this is not the case, and add their signature. If problem behaviour occurs, please fill in the 'Details' section below.

Targets	1	2	3	4	5	6
1 To respond to any reasonable request made by a member of staff.						
2 To remain acceptably on task with work.						
3 To avoid 'shouting out'.						

Signature of Parent/Guardian: _____ Date: _____

Signature of Pastoral Head: _____ Date: _____

Details of any problem behaviour (additional details can be given on reverse)

Date/lesson	What led up to the incident?	What happened?	What were the consequences?	Staff signature

Stage 3

A pupil will move to Stage 3 where behaviour continues to give cause for concern and shows no improvement despite regular reviews that fully involve the parents. It is also possible to *move pupils directly to Stage 3* if the situation warrants it, although this would be the exception.

By this stage it is possible that temporary exclusion may already have been used as a means of signalling the school's disapproval of the pupil's behaviour. Exclusion alone is unlikely to change persistent problem behaviour.

Operation of the code of practice	You will need:
Pupils' behaviour has not been modified by previous measures or behaviour is serious enough to warrant moving directly to Stage 3.	■ some involvement of the educational psychologist in advising generally about the best way to manage this kind of problem behaviour ■ parental permission for the above and involvement of the parent in whatever course of action is suggested ■ further involvement of the SENCO in diagnostic work as appropriate ■ at this stage an agreed contract with the parents and the pupil, together with a revised daily report, may be appropriate. This will both inform and remind all those involved of the pupils' Individual Behaviour Plan and monitor compliance and progress closely. See RB21a and b.

Contract for behaviour management

RB2Ia

Code of Practice Stage 3

Date of commencement:

Date of first review:

Pupil's name: *Pat Jones* Date of birth: *09.07.82*

Reasons for contract:

Pat is a pupil who has been in some trouble recently both for poor behaviour and truancy. Parents visited the school on 4 November 1997 to discuss the situation and to agree a programme to improve behaviour and address truancy.

The School will:

1. *Continue to monitor Pat's progress closely.*
2. *Continue to allow Pat access to a full teaching programme at the school.*
3. *Reward Pat when behaviour is good.*

Mr & Mrs Jones (Parents/Guardians) will:

1. *Check Pat's report card regularly.*
2. *Ensure that Pat is 'grounded' if the day's targets have not been met.*
3. *Will reward Pat if the report is good.*

Pat (Pupil) will:

1. *Work hard to achieve her agreed behavioural targets.*
2. *Will have the report card signed in each registration by the form tutor, and at the end of the day by the Head of Year.*

Signed: _____ (Pastoral Head) Date: _____

Signed: _____ (Parent/Guardian) Date: _____

Signed: _____ (Pupil) Date: _____

Revised IBP Report (RB2lb)

Code of Practice Stage 3

Name of student: _____

Tutor group: _____ Date: _____

Note: Would staff please tick if these targets have been met or put a cross if this is not the case, and add their signature. If problem behaviour occurs, please fill in the 'Details' section below.

Targets	1	2	3	4	5	6
1 To respond to any reasonable request made by a member of staff.						
2 To remain acceptably on task with work.						
3 To avoid 'shouting out'.						
4 To sit on own away from other pupils.						
5 To attend all lessons.						
Achieved all five targets: YES/NO						

Signature of Parent/Guardian: _____ Date: _____

Signature of Pastoral Head: _____ Date: _____

Details of any problem behaviour (additional details can be given on reverse)

Date/lesson	What led up to the incident?	What happened?	What were the consequences?	Staff signature

The nature of the contract and the individual targets set will of course depend on the individual child. Generally, problem behaviour should be divided into its different elements so that the child can make progress in small, achievable steps.

Action at Stage 3 is likely to be more complex and expensive for the school in terms of resources and time allocated to the individual child. However, for a child who might end up permanently excluded it is essential that the school can demonstrate that it has considered all the alternatives and that it has sought professional support through working through the Code of Practice. Appeals against permanent exclusion can include a consideration of whether or not the school has worked through all the available stages.

Stage 4

At Stage 4, the school will normally involve the educational psychologist, who will do an individual assessment of the pupil and provide a specialist behavioural modification programme. This may involve anger management training, referral to a counsellor, or whole-family referral to specialist support. In some areas Pupil Referral Units (PRUs) are available where pupils can have a period away from the mainstream school and can be educated in smaller groups with more individual attention. This is not a long-term answer since the aim of the PRU will be to reintegrate the pupil as soon as practically possible, but it can give both sides a 'breathing space' before further action is taken. Close liaison between the Pastoral Head and the PRU will ensure that the pupil's time at the PRU is well spent.

If a PRU is not available, schools may use a modified timetable in initially placing the pupil only in lessons where they are likely to behave successfully or in changing the timing of the pupil's day so that unstructured break or lunchtimes are taken at a different time from the rest of the school. At this stage a specialist Behaviour Modification Programme needs to be agreed by all parties who need to understand that the situation has reached a very serious stage, with permanent exclusion as the next stage.

Stage 5

A child who reaches Stage 5 is facing permanent exclusion or at least removal into more specialist provision. This is a stage which many schools will work hard to avoid because the future of the child who has been excluded can be bleak. Other schools are reluctant to take pupils who have been excluded elsewhere and it can take some time for the situation to be resolved. In many cases, the most the excluded pupil can hope for is some contact with the Educational Welfare Officer and possibly some home tuition, whilst the LEA considers either an alternative school or alternative provision.

Reviewing or updating the school's behaviour policy

If you do decide that you want to be involved in reviewing or developing the school's behaviour policy, you will need to talk your proposals through with the senior manager responsible for pastoral care. His/her support and involvement in the review process is critical. It is important that any change takes account of the views of:

■ staff
■ pupils
■ parents
■ governors.

To be effective, a whole-school policy should seek the support of all those involved.

One way of initiating change is to set up a working party of interested staff. You will need to have the support of senior management in this, so talk your ideas through with the Head or Deputy Head. The working party should:

■ be open to all members of staff to join
■ include a member of the Senior Management Team to ensure support and communication at the highest level
■ include the SENCO, if possible, since he/she will already be familiar with the Code of Practice.

The starting point for the working party should be some research in the school amongst staff and pupils. For example, the questions on sheet RB22 could form a useful starting point for your discussions.

Behaviour policy checklist (RB22)

- What are the areas of concern shared by both staff and pupils?

- What sort of behaviour is most distracting or unsettling?

- Are procedures understood by all staff and pupils?

- Are sanctions consistently applied?

- Do pupils understand the sanctions and think they are fair?

- Does the school have effective ways of dealing with lower-level misbehaviour as well as major incidents?

- Does problem behaviour rapidly move up to the highest level of management or are there stages in the management of behaviour?

- Is the school actively monitoring and responding to all pupils' behaviour or is it just involved in crisis management?

- When and how are parents involved? Is it at an early stage of any concern or is it only when things are going badly wrong?

- Has the school got the balance of sanctions and rewards right, or is the ethos of the school punitive rather than encouraging?

- How widespread is any problem in the school?

- What do pupils think will make them behave well or work hard?

A questionnaire to staff and pupils will be a useful way of conducting this initial research. This approach should give you a clear idea of where to focus your initial efforts, although in practice you may need to sample the views of pupils rather than dealing with all the responses. The act of asking pupils for their views is, however, a very valuable one, and will help to build a consensus of support for the working party's proposals.

You may find interesting anomalies in your research (e.g. a disparity between the attitudes of pupils and staff about the most effective sanctions). You may also find that the factors that encourage pupils to behave well or work hard are deceptively simple:

- praise
- encouragement
- good teaching
- a good relationship with teachers.

This initial consultation phase with staff and pupils is essential if the working party is to build the necessary support for its later proposals.

Make sure you take full account of the workings of the Code of Practice at this stage. You will want to ensure that your proposals are consistent with its operation to avoid the unnecessary confusion of having two separate systems.

When you put forward your proposal for improvement or change, bear the following points in mind.

- **Consistency is essential.** This means that staff need to fully support and understand what is being proposed. Consistency provides an enormous additional support for staff using the agreed procedures. It establishes and reinforces the clarity of the expectations of behaviour for pupils and ensures that there is more natural justice in the system, which pupils understand and relate to.
- **Positive reinforcement.** Pupils need praise, a sense of achievement and progress and encouragement as much as – some would urge more than – sanctions for misbehaviour.
- **Staged sanctions.** Staging sanctions is important for two reasons. First, because in a classroom situation, misbehaviour usually begins at a lower level and therefore so must the sanctions. Secondly, a staged approach is an essential element of the Code of Practice and whatever form of behaviour policy you adopt, it must integrate with this Code.
- **Monitoring and recording misbehaviour.** Clear, non-emotive records of incidents of misbehaviour are essential, together with a record of the school's responses (see the various forms for this in the Resource Bank). This monitoring and recording is essential so that information is readily available if a temporary or permanent exclusion is considered. It also provides the basis for the necessary monitoring of the application of the Code of Practice.

As part of your behaviour policy review you will want to consider sanctions and rewards.

Sanctions and rewards

Sanctions

In all of your dealings with children, try to remember the old adage, 'Abhor the sin, not the sinner'. Most pupils will accept discipline from adults they believe know and like them, and who are consistent and fair in their application of rules. The ultimate aim for your pupils is self-discipline – so that they can maintain appropriate behaviour even in the absence of external rules and sanctions.

Key factors that promote good behaviour are:

- the example set by adults – staff (teaching and non-teaching) should act with courtesy and respect, particularly in dealing with pupils. Avoid the 'Do as I say, not as I do' style of working
- high expectations of pupils – and not simply in the narrow, academic sense. Make it clear that you have confidence in their ability to act with maturity and to show initiative and consideration for others
- giving young people responsibility – not just in selecting the few for positions as prefects, librarians, etc., but in a sincere expectation that every pupil will accept responsibility in the institution – welcoming visitors, assisting younger pupils, organising the leavers' ball, etc.
- frequent use of praise and encouragement – pupils place this very near the top when asked what motivates them. The Pastoral Head should take every opportunity to dispense praise from the general congratulations in assembly to the quiet word of praise in the corridor
- explaining the reasons for rules – young people do not always see consequences even when we may feel they are obvious. In taking every opportunity to explain rules we show that they exist for good reasons but also that we respect and value our pupils by taking the time and trouble to explain these rules
- consulting pupils about rules – is even more successful if pupils feel they are consulted and have a degree of ownership over school rules. Pupils rarely fail to respond in a mature and thoughtful manner, they are good at updating rules to take account of new circumstances and they particularly enjoy pointing out anomalies that we have not detected.

Negative sanctions serve little purpose – indeed, because they cause resentment they are often counter-productive. Try to bear in mind the following:

- don't set lines, copying from books, etc. They are not only too negative – they are too easy!

- school work should not be associated with punishment. Thus, it is legitimate to require that an unsatisfactory piece of work be repeated, but do not set pages of Maths or an English essay for an unrelated offence
- sarcasm, ridicule and public humiliation will not encourage co-operation
- detention should be used sparingly for serious matters and only where proper procedures have been followed to inform parents, etc. Detention can cause great resentment, especially where it results in problems over transport home or missed activities. Dissuade colleagues from viewing it as something *they* hand out and *you* enforce!

The purpose of imposing a sanction is to encourage the person responsible to:

- register that his/her behaviour has been unacceptable
- understand that he/she has hurt or offended others
- where possible, make some form of restitution (e.g. a letter of apology, paying for, or making a financial contribution towards, damaged or lost property – those found responsible for graffiti should be required to assist caretaking staff in removing it).

Rewards

Many schools have reward systems based on merit points, house points or similar. These can work quite well, especially with younger age groups but they do have drawbacks. Some children become demotivated as the class chart shows them falling further and further behind other pupils. It is difficult to be entirely fair in awarding such points – how does one judge when a child has made a 'special effort'? There is often inconsistency between teachers and systems occasionally lose their credibility. Schemes based on points work best when the points awarded feed into certificates (usually, bronze, silver and gold) or letters home.

Another traditional type of reward is the presentation in school assembly, which is seen as an important incentive by Pastoral Heads and teachers. Unfortunately, there is evidence that suggests that many adolescents do not like to be singled out for praise in front of their peers in this way. You may find it helpful to consult with your pupils and, if necessary, modify your assemblies to take account of their feelings about rewards and recognition.

What young people do value is praise – albeit in private – from a class teacher, tutor or others. As a Pastoral Head, try to insist on hearing good news from your colleagues in at least equal measure to their complaints. Similarly, senior staff, governors and others enjoy the opportunity to praise and commend pupils.

Perhaps the most effective strategy for dealing with both rewards and sanctions is to inform the parents. Try to make it clear to your pupils from the outset those aspects of behaviour that will automatically and inescapably be reported to parents. Many schools and departments have a simple proforma that makes informing parents of their children's good work or effort simple and quick to do. Establishing effective communication and good relationships with parents is, in this area again, the key to success as a Pastoral Head.

Example: One school's behaviour policy

Good behaviour is essential if everyone is to have the opportunity to learn successfully. The **BEST** Code outlines what is expected of all pupils, how they will be encouraged and rewarded, and the staged sanctions which will be used if pupils do not follow the BEST code.

The **BEST** way to learn:

Be prepared for your lessons. Bring books, pens and all necessary equipment.
Expect to learn, and make sure that others are also allowed to learn.
Stay on task. Do not distract yourself or others.
Take homework seriously and hand it in on time.

Rewards

In every lesson where you keep to the BEST code, the teacher will award a BEST stamp. (Stamps to be recorded on special pages in your pupil planner.) When you have achieved a full page of stamps, your form teacher will award you a **BEST** sticker.

When you achieve three **BEST** stickers you will receive a **BEST** Certificate to take home to show your parents. Prizes will also be awarded throughout the year. If you achieve three **BEST** certificates, you will be awarded a Headteacher's Certificate of Achievement and a prize to take home to show your parents.

Sanctions

The pupils, parents and governors of this school believe that every pupil has the right to learn and nobody has the right to disrupt or prevent learning. They have agreed the following staged sanctions to be used if pupils are being prevented from learning.

- **Stage 1**: A clear verbal warning from the teacher telling the pupil that the behaviour is unacceptable.
- **Stage 2**: A second warning and the pupil to be moved (e.g. closer to the teacher or away from other pupils).
- **Stage 3**: Pupil to be put outside the room briefly and his/her behaviour recorded on a pupil referral form. Sanctions (e.g. after-school detention) to be used. Referral form given to form tutor and then to Pastoral Head so that behaviour can be monitored.
- If misbehaviour continues, the pupil will be placed on the Register of Concern and Special Arrangements, and further action involving parents will be taken to change the behaviour. The school has the usual range of sanctions, up to and including permanent exclusion, which is used only as a final resort.

5 The pastoral curriculum

Personal, social, health and careers education

Most Pastoral Heads will be involved to a greater or lesser extent in a Personal, Social and Health Education (PSHE) programme for the pupils in their care. It is important to see such programmes in the context of the broader 'pastoral curriculum', a term first used by Michael Marland in 1981 in *Perspectives on Pastoral Care*.

Schools have always been concerned about the personal and social development of their pupils, whether or not they have used the term 'pastoral curriculum'. However, it has now become common not to leave this personal and social development to chance, but to allocate it time within the school day either in registration time, during assemblies or in timetabled Personal and Social Education lessons. Personal and social education also takes place within the normal school curriculum and there is also what has been called the 'hidden' curriculum of the interaction between the organisation and all the social relationships which exists within it. Thus, the pastoral curriculum encompasses:

- registration time
- assemblies
- timetabled Personal and Social Education courses/tutorial programmes
- personal and social education in the academic curriculum (e.g. health education in Science or Home Economics)

- the 'hidden' curriculum based on the ways pupils are treated by the organisation, by teachers and by each other.

'Personal and social education' is an umbrella term which includes all those areas of personal and social development that the school feels are important and which may or may not also feature in the main curriculum. Thus, it includes:

- specific personal social skills and knowledge
- cross-curricular themes, such as:
  - health education
  - careers education and guidance
  - citizenship education
  - economic and industrial understanding
  - religious and moral/ethical education.

Personal social skills and knowledge

The specific areas of skill or knowledge which relate to the pupils' personal relationships and to their integration and interaction with the school as a community include:

- transition and induction
- coping with bullying
- assertiveness
- self-esteem
- friendships
- personal organisation
- study skills.

Cross-curricular themes

Health education
The government published guidelines on the content of health education and in practice some health education is delivered through the Science, Home Economics and Physical Education provision. It is of course essential to map what is already delivered before including topics in the PSHE programme. Common topics include:

- relationships
- sex education
- alcohol and drugs education
- healthy living.

Careers education and guidance

Common themes include:

- the development of knowledge of opportunities and different qualification routes
- the development of self-awareness
- the development of decision-making in relation to career choice
- the provision of continuous, individual and impartial careers guidance
- the development of personal and social skills, including study skills, to manage the transition from school to adult and working life.

Citizenship education

This might include:

- legal rights and responsibilities
- the role of the police
- understanding the local community
- local and national policies
- social support organisations
- concern for the environment.

Economic and industrial understanding

This is often subsumed under the heading of Careers Education and Guidance and can include work experience, work-based learning, industrial simulations and understanding industry activities.

Religious and moral/ethical education

- The Education Reform Act of 1988 outlines that the curriculum of a maintained school must 'promote the spiritual, moral, cultural, mental and physical development of pupils'.
- Many schools therefore teach Religious Education as part of the curriculum, and many also include moral issues such as abortion or euthanasia in their PSHE programme. Most schools also insist on a code of behaviour with at least an implicit ethical stance.
- However, Michael Marland has highlighted the fact that there is little attempt in most schools to map the relationship between the requirement for 'moral' development, the compulsory religious education component of the curriculum and the insistence on school behaviour with ethical principles. His argument that 'ethical and value issues lie at the heart of the school' is likely to have real meaning to Pastoral Heads who deal with such issues in a practical and developmental setting every day of the week.

Schools often deliver aspects of their pastoral curriculum through a timetabled tutorial programme. An example of the content of one recent tutorial programme (PSHE) in an 11–16 high school is shown below, but all schools vary to some degree in their choice of topics and the emphasis given to them.

Year 7	Year 8	Year 9
■ Induction. ■ Study skills 1: Organising your homework. ■ Getting to know yourself. ■ Managing friendships. ■ Working as a team. ■ Bullying 1. ■ Health education 1: Personal hygiene. ■ Health education 2: Healthy eating. ■ Moral issues 1: Poverty, hunger and malnutrition. ■ Health education 3: Water safety.	■ Health education 3: Smoking. ■ Community police officer: Self-defence lessons. ■ Moral issues 2: Personal organisation. ■ The environment: does it matter? ■ Personal safety: On the streets. ■ Health education 4: Alcohol. ■ Moral issues 3: Right and wrong. ■ Study skills 3: Revision skills. ■ Care for the community: vandalism. ■ Bullying 2.	■ Careers education: All about me. ■ Careers education: Introduction to careers library. ■ Careers education: Option choices. ■ Health education 5: Substance abuse – drugs and the law. ■ Careers education: Personal skills and job skills. ■ Bullying 3. ■ Health education 6: First aid and resuscitation. ■ Health education 7: Safety on the railway. ■ Moral issues: Euthanasia. ■ Health education 8: Sexual responsibility and sexual health.

Year 10	Year 11	
■ Careers education: Computer-based programmes. ■ Bullying 4. ■ Drugs awareness: The life of the addict. ■ Economic and industrial understanding: Work simulations and understanding. Industry days. ■ Study skills 4: Preparing for public exams. ■ Moral issues: Crime and punishment. ■ Community police officer: Joy-riding. ■ Moral issues: Prejudice and tolerance. ■ Records of achievement.	■ Careers education: Preparation for work experience. ■ Work experience. Qualification framework and where to study. ■ Study Skills 5: Revision skills. ■ Health education: Sex education and parenting issues. ■ Careers education: Further Education courses. ■ Record of achievement. ■ Moral issues: Abortion. ■ Careers education: CVs and letters of application. Interview skills. ■ Moral issues: Equality of opportunity.	

Planning the pastoral curriculum

The pastoral curriculum can be one of the key ways in which the school transmits its values, aims and ethos to pupils. For example, if the school aims to develop all pupils to their full potential, and therefore values individuality, the pastoral curriculum can give expression to this by providing pupils with individual guidance interviews, records of achievement, and personal mentors. It is worth giving this some thought before setting about designing a pastoral or tutorial programme. The following completed planning form is an example of such preparatory work.

Pastoral curriculum planning form 1 (RB23)

School aim	Values/beliefs	Topic	Activity
To enable students to develop to their full potential	*Belief in the value of individual talents.*	■ *Records of achievement.* ■ *Individual guidance interviews.* ■ *Personal mentors.*	■ *Pupils working individually on their own RoA.* ■ *Individual interview with Careers Officer.* ■ *Personal mentor assigned to each individual to monitor progress in exam year and offer support.* ■ *Individual pupil's achievement recognised and rewarded (e.g. in assembly).*
	Belief in equality of opportunity.	■ *Equal opportunities.*	■ *Lessons in equal opportunities/ discrimination, etc.*
	Belief that pupils must not be threatened or upset by other pupils to the detriment of their individual progress.	■ *Bullying.* ■ *Assertiveness.*	■ *Lessons to encourage pupils to report bullying and to become assertive.* ■ *Assemblies in which pupils act out bullying situations to enable pupils to think through the issues.*

There is a blank grid (RB23) in the Resource Bank at the back of the book to enable you to do this exercise with colleagues at the stage you are planning your assemblies and tutorial programme.

Sometimes school assembly topics and the personal and social education programme are planned separately, even though they involve the pastoral curriculum for the same group of pupils and are delivered by the same Pastoral Head and tutor team. It is helpful, however, to see assemblies, registration times and Personal, Social and Health Education lessons as an integrated way of delivering the pastoral curriculum and to plan all three together, relating them to the aims of the school and the aims of the pastoral curriculum.

School aim	Related pastoral curriculum aim	Week no.	Registration time	Assembly theme	PSE programme
To prepare pupils for life and work in the 21st century.	To provide all pupils with careers education and guidance. To develop personal organisation skills.	1 2 3 4 5 etc.	Use of careers library or computer-based careers programmes. Use of personal planners.	Differences between school and outside world. Planning ahead.	Introduction to different job families and skill requirements Introduction to study skills – homework.

A planning grid like the one below will help you with this. A copy of this grid is provided in the Resource Bank (RB24) at the back of the book.

Pastoral curriculum planning form 2 (RB24)

YEAR:	TERM:				
School aim	Related pastoral curriculum aim	Week no.	Registration time	Assembly theme	PSE programme

To begin to plan the pastoral curriculum you will therefore need to:

- take account of the overall school aims
- identify aims for the pastoral curriculum which support the school's aims
- think broadly about the way in which the pastoral curriculum can be delivered (e.g. assemblies, registration time, tutorial or PSHE lessons, within the normal curriculum)
- map any areas that are currently partly delivered in the curriculum (e.g. health education)
- be perceptive about the 'hidden' curriculum. For example, it would be difficult to develop self-esteem through the tutorial programme if the way pupils are grouped or treated within the school structure deprives them of self-esteem. Likewise lessons on equality may have little impact in a school that provides some of its pupils with better teachers or a wider choice in the curriculum than others.

Try to establish a team of staff to help in the planning of the programme, both to share the workload and to make use of different areas of expertise. A planning team might include:

- the Pastoral Head
- the Head of Careers Education
- the Careers Officer
- the teacher responsible for health education
- other interested staff.

Any planning for a year group must however also take account of the development of the programme in other years. Ideally, the whole school programme is planned in outline first, with resources and rooms identified, and then detailed planning takes place within the year or house team. Planning sheets like the ones below are useful here and copies of these planning sheets are included in the Resource Bank at the back of this book.

Tutorial/PSHE planning form 1 (RB25)
– whole-school outline

Term	Wk	Year 7 Topic	Year 8 Topic	Year 9 Topic	Year 10 Topic	Year 11 Topic
ONE	1					
	2					
	3					
	4					
	5					
	6					
	7					
	8					
	9					
	10					
	11					
	12					
	13					
	14					
TWO	15					
	16					
	17					
	18					
	19					
	20					
	21					
	22					
	23					
	24					
	25					
	26					
	27					
	28					
	29					
	30					
THREE	31					
	32					
	33					
	34					
	35					
	36					
	37					
	38					
	39					
	40					
	41					
	42					
	43					
	44					
	45					

The programme should be planned for the whole year and should also take account of the cycle of school events and activities. Usually, it is possible to begin to outline planning in May and then start detailed planning in June when the calendar for the following year becomes available. Using a detailed planning sheet, you will need to produce individual lesson plans since tutors need to work to a common format. It is essential that you:

- involve tutors in the design of the overall programme and agree lesson plans
- take account of the demands of the academic year (e.g. examinations, reports)
- plan your programme in the broader context of the school's overall aims and programmes.

Tutorial/PSHE planning form 2 (RB26) – room use planner

Term	Wk	Room: Year: Form:	Room: Year: Form:	Room: Year: Form:	Room: Year: Form:	Room: Year: Form:
ONE	1 2 3 4 5 6 7 8 9 10 11 12 13 14					
TWO	15 16 17 18 19 20 21 22 23 24 25 26 27 28 29 30					
THREE	31 32 33 34 35 36 37 38 39 40 41 42 43 44 45					

Date	Week no.	Lesson activity	Resources	Staff	Venue	Notes

Assemblies and spiritual and moral development

Assemblies present a challenge for Pastoral Heads and must be planned with care. A daily act of worship is a legal requirement and at least 50 per cent of this must be of a broadly Christian nature. In many schools, children from practising Christian families will be in the minority. In some areas most pupils will be Muslim or Hindu. It is important that the school, through the Pastoral Head, shows respect for these traditions. A good way is to ensure that the pattern of assemblies planned includes the most important festivals from the other main religions. Links can be made with the mosque, Hindu or Sikh temple, as well as the local Christian churches. With effort and planning a varied programme can be put together which is spiritually uplifting, informative and fulfils the legal requirements.

The Pastoral Head should ensure that all parents are aware that they may withdraw their children from assemblies. This might be taken up not only by followers of religions other than Christianity but by Christians such as Jehovah's Witnesses. Particularly in non-church schools, practising Christians will sometimes withdraw their children from assembly because they do not regard it as a genuine act of worship. Children withdrawn from assembly are still the responsibility of the school. Ideally, they should be supervised in a room suitable for quiet contemplation but close to the assembly room so that they may unobtrusively join the group for notices, sports results, etc. Remember that some of these children may suffer embarrassment or worse if they are perceived of as being different. Treat them with consideration and watch for signs of ridicule or bullying.

The OFSTED guidance on inspection tells us that, 'evaluation should focus on whether acts of worship . . . encourage pupils to explore questions about meaning and purpose, values and beliefs'. Most teachers would accept that, though difficult, this is a task in which they should, as educators in the broadest sense, be involved. If the Pastoral Head sees assembly as raising the questions rather than providing the answers then, with effort and imagination, assemblies can be planned which engage young people, get them thinking and participating and satisfy the legal requirements.

Assemblies – a practical guide

Leading assemblies

Appointment to a pastoral post will usually mean taking on responsibility for leading assemblies, often for the first time. Taking a house or year assembly can be quite a challenge but it can also be a very rewarding experience. It gives the Pastoral Head the chance to lead and influence pupils (and staff) and to develop and strengthen the ethos of the group. For this reason, it is important that anyone seeking a pastoral post develops expertise and experience in taking assemblies, either as a tutor on a rotational basis, or by observing a senior colleague and building up to a leading role. Careful preparation and a professional approach will carry most Pastoral Heads through the early experience of leading an assembly. In time, a genuine rapport can be developed with the year group, with the Pastoral Head taking a leading role in transmitting the values and expectations of the school to the pupils.

Material for assemblies

There are many assembly books and folders on the market (see, for example, the Heinemann Assembly Resource series), some even have accompanying music and video tapes. These can be a useful source though usually need to be tailored to the particular circumstances of the school. Some of the best sources of subjects for assembly are daily and Sunday newspapers. From global conflict to local disputes between neighbours, from lottery winners to pet rescuers, newspapers offer a wealth of stories, written in a style and using language that young people find accessible.

As an example, hardly a month goes by without a report on the latest ideas regarding the origins of the universe. The bare facts about the universe are so dramatic and impressive they rarely fail to grip the young audience. They lead on quite naturally to questions of meaning and purpose and, in these circumstances, explanations offered by world religions do not seem out of place.

Articles from newspapers and magazines offer excellent opportunities to contribute not only to the spiritual aspect but also other aspects of pupils' development as described in the OFSTED guidance:

- to teach the principles which distinguish right from wrong
- to encourage pupils to relate positively to others, take responsibility, participate fully in the community and develop an understanding of citizenship
- to teach pupils to appreciate their own cultural traditions and the diversity and richness of other cultures.

> **Start with the story, explain the issue it illustrates, make the link with the pupils' own situations and experiences.**

You may find it helpful to plan some of the main assembly themes in discussion with your team, using a planner like the one shown below, which is also contained in the Resource Bank.

Assembly planner (RB28)

Month	Dates to note	Assembly themes	Readings/materials
Sept.	Start of academic year Rosh Hashanah ↓		
Oct.			
Nov.	11th – Armistice Day Remembrance Sunday 30th – St Andrew's Day		
Dec.	25th – Christmas		
Jan.	New Year Ramadan		
Feb.			
March	1st – St David's Day 17th St Patrick's Day Easter ↓		
April	23rd – St George's Day		
May	May Day		
June			
July	4th – USA Independence Day		
Aug.			

Managing staff support in assemblies

In organising your assemblies with staff:

- it may not be popular, but insist that all tutors attend every assembly. Use senior management to support your stance if necessary. There is no reason why staff, excused from assemblies on religious grounds, should not still come in to hear notices

- encourage tutors to take turns in leading their own assembly. This takes some of the pressure off you and, at the very least, will make them less critical of your efforts!

- from time to time place assemblies on your agenda for team meetings, not simply to arrange dates and themes but to discuss the important values that should be brought out, how you might work together and also to consider pupil responses

- establish procedures, including tutors moving to the assembly room with their groups (not ahead of them or, more commonly, bringing up the rear with several colleagues) and sitting with them when they arrive. This is part of the collective responsibility for how pupils move around the school and the establishment of an appropriate atmosphere in the assembly room

- make an opportunity to walk around tutor rooms and corridors to ensure your procedures are being followed – ideally on an occasion when someone else is leading the assembly

- assign responsibilities to all members of the tutor team. Those without a tutor group of their own should be particularly useful, perhaps getting to the assembly room first to ensure the right atmosphere on entry, or immediately outside the assembly room, directing the flow of pupils through available doors or the storage of school bags and coats. Tutors who register close to the assembly area should be used in a similar way, whilst those further away, and therefore last to arrive, can be used to hurry dawdlers and, if necessary, check nearby toilets or other places of refuge!

Managing pupils' contribution to assemblies

As with other aspects of school life, pupils gain most value from assemblies in which they participate. Form assemblies are important team building opportunities – the chance for all pupils to bring out their own ideas and talents as readers and actors. Pupils often listen more attentively to their peers and genuinely appreciate the effort that others are making in performing the assembly. In this way, they often come to a better understanding of the complexities of life and more readily explore the spiritual dimension.

Younger children have few inhibitions about involvement in front of their peers but teenagers may see such activity as 'uncool' and potentially embarrassing. The practice is best established upon entry to the school building upon the participation and enjoyment established in many primary schools. As the pupils grow older they may become less enthusiastic, at least on the surface, but the strength of the tradition and the expectation built up will carry them through. Remember that teenage reluctance is often superficial. As with most other aspects of school life, leadership, enthusiasm and setting an example are central to your success.

When arranging pupil assemblies:

- encourage pupils to come up with their own ideas and themes which then leaves you with the task of trying to fit these ideas into a spiritual and moral framework
- make sure pupils understand the importance of seeing things through, even a short assembly demands more time, effort and practice than pupils expect at the outset
- make sure pupils are aware of parameters of time, space and resources. The impact of a brilliantly conceived assembly can be lost if it overruns by even a few minutes
- remember that pupils cannot be expected to manage the whole process without help. A supportive and tactful adult should stay as much in the background as possible but always be ready to step into an area of dispute, saving valuable time and teenage pride!

Managing the accommodation

One of the first requisites of a successful assembly is to create the right atmosphere. Many school halls lend themselves well to this but house and year assemblies often take place in any space large enough to accommodate the group (e.g. sports hall, gymnasium, dining room or large classroom). Extraneous noise, cramped conditions (or the reverse – a space far larger than required), or lack of adequate seating are some of the factors that make getting the right 'feel' more difficult. Nevertheless, a little ingenuity can substantially improve the atmosphere and suitability of any area. Good organisation, enthusiasm, confidence, sincerity in delivery and the support of the tutor team can make for successful assemblies even in the least promising of circumstances.

Example

The venue is a sports hall with the problem that the space available is much too large for the year group using it for assembly. The Head of Year has used two trampolines (TR) and four table tennis tables (TTT), in their upright storage positions, to create a feeling of enclosing the assembly in an appropriate sized space.

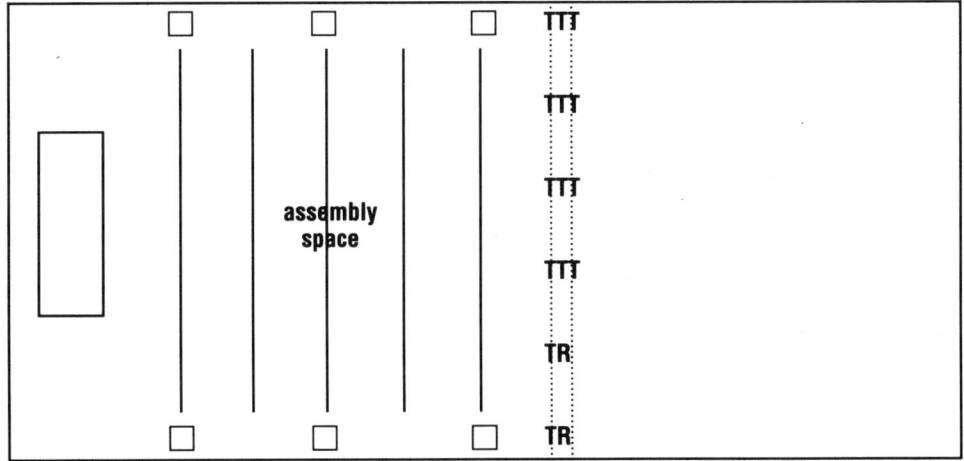

Policy formulation and evaluation

Pastoral policy

The benefits of a pastoral policy are twofold:

1 the process of policy development involves all staff in full consultation and discussion of the pastoral aims of the school and in their implementation
2 a written policy offers a valuable reference point against which to plan, implement and monitor progress.

An effective policy should detail the following:

- the background and need for the policy
- the pastoral goals of the school
- the policy in practice: structures, roles, tasks, curriculum, procedures, etc.
- resources to support the policy, including money, staff and time
- action to be taken, by whom and when
- appropriate dissemination of the policy
- arrangements for monitoring and reviewing the policy.

PASTORAL POLICY I

Langland School is committed to the development and growth of the whole child, and does not see a divide between the pupil's intellectual progression and his/her development as a caring member of the school community.

The school places a very high value on the partnerships developed between staff, parents and pupils to ensure that progress is as successful as possible. Success at Langland is based upon the premise of creating a well-ordered environment in which learning can flourish and where responsibility for one's own actions and having respect for each other is clearly understood. We strive to ensure that our pupils develop as moral, self-reflective members of the school community.

We believe in the right balance of control and freedom by the use of a firm but fair reinforcement system which emphasises good behaviour. We set high standards for pupils in work, behaviour and attendance in an atmosphere which is warm, friendly and caring.

Our reward system supports achievement in the fullest sense; academic, pastoral and community service. Pupils have the opportunity to participate in decision-making through their year meetings and school council.

Classroom relationships, communication systems, extra-curricular activities and the many forms of discussion between teacher and teacher, and teacher and pupils are as much a part of our pastoral care as the formal tutor periods, record of achievement sessions and personal development lessons.

All staff at our school have an understanding of pupils' pastoral needs, but two groups have a very particular responsibility. A pupil's form tutor will be the teacher he/she sees every day, who will respond to problems and keep a caring eye on progress. The tutors will usually remain with their forms for their five years of schooling at Langland. Form tutors are also able to spend additional time with their forms during timetabled form periods and one-to-one review interviews take place twice a year on our Record of Achievement Days. For parents and pupils, the form tutor is the first point of contact with the school. This contact is the core of the trusting, caring relationship which supports the pupil's progress during his/her school life. Naturally, parents, pupils and form tutors may wish to send parents a message by writing in pupils' diaries. After consultation with year tutors, form tutors may also wish to write to parents or telephone them. There is a great deal of consultation about pupils between form tutors and year tutors. In this way, good communication and close relationships can be established throughout the five years.

The year tutors lead teams of form tutors and frame the year's form activities to suit the development of their respective years. The tutor has an overview of the taught content of personal development and form periods, takes a weekly assembly and also deals with issues concerned with the development of individual pupils or groups of pupils.

The Deputy Head has overall responsibility for the pastoral process. She also supports individual pupils and colleagues regarding matters of particular sensitivity, and works closely with year tutors and Heads of Department should there be whole-school implications.

PASTORAL POLICY 2

In our pastoral work at Caswell School, we seek to create a community that develops self-respect in our students, leading to a respect for others, whatever their perceived difference, and the environment. This is based on a mutual respect between staff and students and we seek to provide positive role models for students during a period of powerful identity development.

As a school, we exist to enable each student to reach his/her potential as a human being and we, therefore, seek to create an orderly, safe, supportive and even affectionate atmosphere where all may thrive.

We hope to show each student that actions have consequences – a kind of 'do-as-you-would-be-done-by' philosophy – but further that we are all part of a common whole and all gain from positive input and are adversely affected by negative actions.

Staff and students work together in partnership with parents and the broader community to prepare young citizens who may carry with them the memory of a successful community where violence, discrimination and a disregard for the environment were facets of an outside world, unacceptable in the Caswell oasis.

Monitoring and evaluation

Below are some key questions to enable you to carry out ongoing monitoring and evaluation of your pastoral responsibilities either as part of an internal review or as a preparation for external inspection. This activity is of greatest benefit when performed as a team exercise. The main purpose of the activity is to enable you and your team to produce robust evidence to demonstrate success in the respective areas. Put another way, you and the team should take each item in turn and ask, 'How do we know?'

Pupils' attitudes, behaviour and personal development

Pupils:

- show interest in their work
- are able to sustain concentration
- demonstrate a capacity for personal study
- behave well in and around the school
- are courteous
- are trustworthy
- show respect for property
- form constructive relationships with one another

- form constructive relationships with teachers
- form constructive relationships with other adults
- work collaboratively when required
- show respect for other people's feelings, values and beliefs
- show initiative and are willing to take responsibility.

Possible sources of evidence:
- school policy on behaviour and discipline
- observation around school
- classroom observation
- code of conduct
- referrals and exclusions procedures
- discussions with pupils
- discussions with parents, teachers, governors.

Attendance and punctuality

The school ensures that:

- attendance is a high priority
- the legal requirements for recording and reporting attendance are met
- high attendance rates are promoted and maintained
- support is provided for pupils who return to school after a period of absence
- procedures are in place for noting pupils' absence and for the appropriate follow-up action
- discrepancies between attendance figures in year/class groups are investigated
- procedures are in place for liaising with parents and EWO
- pupils come to school on time
- pupils arrive at lessons on time.

Possible sources of evidence:
- sampling of registers
- analysis of attendance records
- lesson observation
- discussions with staff, pupils, etc.
- policy documents
- reward schemes
- EWO records.

Spiritual, moral, social and cultural development

The school:

- has a clear philosophy, values and principles which underpin pastoral care
- provides pupils with knowledge and insight into values and beliefs
- enables pupils to reflect on their experiences in a way that develops their spiritual awareness and self-knowledge
- teaches the principles that distinguish right from wrong
- encourages pupils to relate positively to others
- encourages pupils to take responsibility
- encourages pupils to participate fully in the community
- encourages pupils to develop an understanding of citizenship
- teaches pupils to appreciate their own cultural traditions
- teaches pupils the diversity and richness of other cultures.

Possible sources of evidence:
- school aims, objectives and policies
- the whole curriculum including religious education
- discussions with pupils
- discussions with staff, governors, parents
- observation of all aspects of the life of the school
- assemblies and collective worship
- sanctions and rewards systems
- code of conduct
- levels of involvement in extra-curricular activities
- pupils' relationships with peers, staff and other adults.

Pupils' welfare and guidance

The school:

- has a clear policy for identifying pupils' needs and monitoring their progress
- provides effective support and advice for all pupils
- provides structured guidance at key transition points (e.g. Year 9 and Year 11)
- publishes job descriptions which clearly define the roles of tutors and Pastoral Heads

- allocates time for pastoral staff to interview pupils and parents
- effectively monitors pupils' academic progress
- effectively monitors pupils' personal development
- effectively monitors pupils' behaviour
- effectively monitors pupils' attendance and punctuality
- has effective measures for promoting discipline and good behaviour
- has effective measures for eliminating oppressive behaviour (e.g. bullying)
- has effective child protection procedures
- successfully promotes the health, safety and general well-being of its pupils
- makes effective and efficient use of support agencies.

Possible sources of evidence:
- guidance policy
- pastoral policy/guidelines
- careers policy/guidelines
- timetable
- job descriptions of tutors and Pastoral Heads
- record of involvement of agencies
- discussions with pupils
- pupil shadowing
- discussions with parents
- lesson observation
- discussion with staff.

Partnerships with parents and the community

The school:

- promotes links with parents that contribute to pupils' learning
- makes good use of brochures, newsletters, etc., to communicate its philosophy and ethos to parents and the wider community
- works in partnership with parents and the community, including employers
- has a policy for supporting new intake pupils and pupils who are transferring
- ensures that, on transfer, information concerning pupils'

achievements and progress is clearly presented in a useful format
- has an effective policy for liaising with feeder and receiving schools/colleges
- provides effective work experience for its pupils
- promotes pupils' contributions to the local community
- ensures that its links with the community offer pupils a means of extending their education experience beyond the classroom.

Possible sources of evidence:
- communication and feedback from parents
- school prospectus and other documentation
- parents' consultation meetings
- primary school liaison
- transfer and new intake information
- discussion on continuity and progression issues
- work experience placements
- career conventions
- pupils' work
- community use of school's resources.

Resource Bank

Sample job description

POST: Head of Year

Under the general direction of the Headteacher, the Year Head has responsibility for the pastoral care and academic progress of a cohort of students. He/she therefore has the following duties and responsibilities:

1 To get to know students in the year group as well as possible and to become accepted as a person to whom they can turn for guidance in addition to their form tutor.

2 To monitor the progress of students. To insist on high standards of co-operation and behaviour and to initiate action when these are unsatisfactory, using strategies such as the Year Heads' Report System, counselling, detention, etc. School policy requires that parents are involved in pastoral and disciplinary matters at an early stage.

3 In discussion with form tutors, Head of Careers and Deputy Heads, to direct and organise a programme of tutorial work for students.

4 To be a member of the Year Heads' Committee and to work with the Senior Management Team to develop appropriate policies and procedures for the effective pastoral care of all students.

5 To lead a team of form tutors, ensuring through regular minuted meetings that all members of the team understand the policies of the school as well as making the Senior Management Team aware of the tutors' views and of the tutor teams' ideas for development. Proposals may be placed on the Year Heads' Agenda for consideration across the whole school.

6 To ensure, by attendance at meetings and regular briefings, that the Headteacher and members of the Senior Management Team are kept informed of matters pertaining to the year group, academic progress, co-operation, attendance, etc.

7 To co-ordinate all information received from staff, parents and outside agencies regarding individual students. To ensure this information is distributed correctly and to check that action is taken where and when necessary.

8 To be responsible for the maintenance of appropriate records, including students' individual files, and to ensure that these are passed on when students transfer.

9 To organise the preparation of reports, records of achievement and references, including confidential court/social service/medical reports.

10 To participate in liaison arrangements with other phases of the student's education, contributory Middle Schools, Year 12/13 and Further Education colleges.

11 To be responsible for the operation of the school's Special Needs Code of Practice as it pertains to behavioural aspects, including appropriate documentation, liaison with SENCO and the Deputy Head with responsibility for Learning Support.

Self-evaluation questionnaire  RB2

Rate your performance using the scale:
1= very good 2 = good 3 = satisfactory 4 = some weakness 5 = area for improvement

Be honest with yourself – and don't underestimate your abilities!

		1	2	3	4	5
1	Ability to communicate with members of the pastoral team	☐	☐	☐	☐	☐
2	Ability to communicate ideas in writing	☐	☐	☐	☐	☐
3	Ability to communicate ideas orally	☐	☐	☐	☐	☐
4	Ability to represent the views of the pastoral team to SMT	☐	☐	☐	☐	☐
5	Ability to represent the views of SMT to the pastoral team	☐	☐	☐	☐	☐
6	Ability to organise the administration of pastoral care	☐	☐	☐	☐	☐
7	Ability to delegate responsibilities to others within the team	☐	☐	☐	☐	☐
8	Ability to listen to the views of pupils and staff	☐	☐	☐	☐	☐
9	Ability to influence and motivate pupils	☐	☐	☐	☐	☐
10	Ability to chair pastoral team meetings	☐	☐	☐	☐	☐
11	Ability to handle difficult members of the team	☐	☐	☐	☐	☐
12	Ability to provide constructive criticism	☐	☐	☐	☐	☐
13	Ability to accept constructive criticism	☐	☐	☐	☐	☐
14	Ability to plan ahead and set realistic targets for pastoral development	☐	☐	☐	☐	☐
15	Ability to implement agreed plans	☐	☐	☐	☐	☐
16	Ability to solve problems	☐	☐	☐	☐	☐
17	Ability to use time effectively	☐	☐	☐	☐	☐
18	Ability to manage stress	☐	☐	☐	☐	☐
19	Ability to identify priorities	☐	☐	☐	☐	☐
20	Ability to understand whole-school issues	☐	☐	☐	☐	☐

Team leader checklist

What kind of team leader are you?

Ask yourself the following questions:

- Have I allocated the tutor groups fairly? — Yes ☐ No ☐

- Have I delegated routine duties, chores, creative tasks and projects appropriately? — Yes ☐ No ☐

- Have I allowed some scope for tutors to be creative/independent decision-makers? — Yes ☐ No ☐

- Does each tutor have a clear description of his/her role? — Yes ☐ No ☐

- Do I know the strengths, weaknesses, concerns and aspirations of my tutors? — Yes ☐ No ☐

- Is there opportunity for regular individual review? — Yes ☐ No ☐

- Do I discuss with each tutor his/her professional development/INSET requirements? — Yes ☐ No ☐

- Do I balance individual needs against the needs of the whole team? — Yes ☐ No ☐

- Have I set achievable targets for the year? — Yes ☐ No ☐

- Do I consult with the team and accept their advice? — Yes ☐ No ☐

- Do I keep the team fully informed? — Yes ☐ No ☐

- How well do I explain their case to the Senior Management Team? — well ⌐—┴—┴—┴—┐ not well

- Do they have adequate resources to carry out their tasks? — Yes ☐ No ☐

- How well have I presented my personal/the school's philosophy to the team? — well ⌐—┴—┴—┴—┐ not well

The Pastoral Head's Handbook © Heinemann Educational Publishers

Year planner

Jan.	Feb.	March	April	May	June	July	Aug.	Sept.	Oct.	Nov.	Dec.

Daily planner

Date:	
Before school	Notes
Break	Notes
Lunch	Notes
After school	Notes

The Pastoral Head's Handbook © Heinemann Educational Publishers.

Personal planner

Subject	Action to be taken	Deadline	Follow-up

The Pastoral Heads Handbook © Heinemann Educational Publishers.

Priority planner

Week commencing: _____

Urgent	Important	Long term	Other

The Pastoral Head's Handbook © Heinemann Educational Publishers

Pastoral team meeting checklist

Before the meeting

1 Have you planned to include longer-term policy issues as well as more immediate issues in your meeting? Yes ☐ No ☐

2 Have you asked for contributions to the agenda from the pastoral team and others? Yes ☐ No ☐

3 Have you circulated the agenda, notes of previous meeting and relevant papers in advance of the meeting? Yes ☐ No ☐

4 Have you arranged a suitable venue where all can be comfortable and take an active part in the meeting? Yes ☐ No ☐

5 Have you arranged for refreshments? Yes ☐ No ☐

At the meeting

6 Did you ensure that someone was appointed to record decisions/action points? Yes ☐ No ☐

7 Did you ensure that the seating arrangements allowed everyone to contribute? Yes ☐ No ☐

8 Did you check the accuracy of the previous minutes and allow matters arising to be raised? Yes ☐ No ☐

9 Did you prevent one or more colleagues from dominating the meeting? Yes ☐ No ☐

10 Did you ask for contributions from the quieter members of the group? Yes ☐ No ☐

11 Did you check that everyone understood the nature of any decisions taken? Yes ☐ No ☐

12 Did you keep the meeting to time? Yes ☐ No ☐

13 Did you cover the agenda? Yes ☐ No ☐

Sample job description

POST: Form tutor

The form tutor plays a very important role in the school, aiming to establish close relationships with the pupils in his/her care and getting to know them as individuals.

Together with the Head of Year the tutor takes an active lead in building the link between home and school, consulting with parents as the need arises.

The form tutor's responsibilities include:

1 Monitoring pupils' attendance

- Contacting home when absences are unexplained after a period of two days.
- Ensuring the prompt receipt of letters from parents explaining absence.
- Sending out the standardised request for an explanation if not forthcoming.
- Alerting the Head of Year to any problems or concerns regarding attendance.

2 Monitoring standards of appearance

- Ensuring that the correct items of uniform are worn.
- Ensuring that jewellery, make-up, etc. is not being worn.

3 Monitoring standards of behaviour

Helping to ensure that standards of behaviour are upheld by encouraging pupils to follow the School Code.

4 Homework

Checking homework journals regularly to ensure that these are kept up to date and signed by parents.

5 Disseminating information

Ensuring that published communications from school to home are effectively distributed and returns collected as necessary.

6 The PSHE Programme

Although the Head of Year provides the structure for the PSHE Programme, it is the tutor who plays the major role in interpreting and delivering the programme. Tutor evaluation of the programme is most valuable as part of the review process.

7 Profiling and reporting procedure

The tutor's role in profiling is an essential and demanding one in terms of organisation and implementation of the procedure. The tutor's skills in counselling and interviewing are integral to the profiling procedure. Increasingly, the profiling process will become an established part of the PSHE Programme. Good communication between the tutor, subject teachers, Head of Year and Senior Management is essential in order to ensure that any individual problems are resolved as effectively as possible.

8 Assemblies and reflection time

The tutor is responsible for ensuring that students move promptly and silently to assembly on the appropriate days. The tutor is also responsible for drawing up a schedule for the form to plan its reflection time in line with the guidelines.

Induction planning checklist

1 Have you made a preliminary visit to all the feeder schools?   Yes ☐   No ☐

2 Have you made arrangements for the transfer of academic information?   Yes ☐   No ☐

3 Have you agreed a common format for the transfer of academic information?   Yes ☐   No ☐

4 Have you made arrangements for the transfer of personal, medical or sensitive information?   Yes ☐   No ☐

5 Have you considered how this information will be transmitted to other staff?   Yes ☐   No ☐

6 Have you made arrangements for all important information about pupils' prior attainment and personal circumstances to be passed on to subject teachers?   Yes ☐   No ☐

7 Have you planned an induction day or session for new pupils?   Yes ☐   No ☐

8 Do all staff, including non-teaching staff, know what your plans are for the induction day?   Yes ☐   No ☐

9 Have you planned an evening for parents to meet their child's new tutor?   Yes ☐   No ☐

10 Have you planned a follow-up evening for parents early in the Autumn Term to follow up any initial concerns?   Yes ☐   No ☐

Ten further ways to improve attendance and punctuality – a checklist

1 Have you checked your guidelines? You may be recording as absence something which other schools count as attendance (e.g. work experience, fieldwork, etc.). Yes ☐ No ☐

2 Have you stressed the importance of good attendance and punctuality through assemblies? (Remember not to nag though – it can be counter-productive!) Yes ☐ No ☐

3 Have you sent parents a clear explanation of the importance of good attendance, and what you are doing to improve attendance rates? Yes ☐ No ☐

4 Have you made it clear to pupils and parents that medical and dental appointments should not be in school time? Do you insist that if such appointments are unavoidable, the pupil attends before/after the appointment? Yes ☐ No ☐

5 Do you ensure that form tutors receive an explanation for all absence and late arrival and do you occasionally take a random sample of pupils to follow up their reasons for yourself? (Remember to use the Education Welfare Officer to follow up the more persistent problems, and be prepared to challenge and disbelieve parents on occasions. You may not be popular but you will secure improvement.) Yes ☐ No ☐

6 Have you set up incentive schemes such as rewards, letters home or certificates for good attendance or punctuality? (These can have a significant effect, especially when built up over time.) Yes ☐ No ☐

7 Have you considered the example set by colleagues? Are there certain issues which senior management should be raising with certain individuals either about their own attendance and punctuality, or about condoning the absence of some of the more difficult pupils? Yes ☐ No ☐

8 Are you aware of any pupils working illegally or just working long hours to the detriment of their education and attendance? Yes ☐ No ☐

9 Are you aware of using employers constructively to stress the importance of good attendance and punctuality? Yes ☐ No ☐

10 Is the work ethic of the school a positive one, or do lessons start late or finish early; does little work happen on the last day of term, etc.? Yes ☐ No ☐

The Pastoral Head's Handbook © Heinemann Educational Publishers

Incident report form

NAME: YEAR:

DATE: TIME:

DETAILS OF INCIDENT:

Signed:

> *For staff use only*
>
>
>
>
>
> Signed:

Bullying report form

Please fill in and pass this to the form tutor of any child involved in *any* incident of bullying. The form tutor will ensure that it is passed to the Pastoral Head.

NAME: YEAR:

DATE: TIME:

DETAILS OF INCIDENT:

ACTION TAKEN:

Signed:_____

Form tutor comment/action:

Pastoral Head comment/action:

The Pastoral Head's Handbook © Heinemann Educational Publishers

Log of bullying incidents

Date	Year group	No. of pupils involved		Nature of incident		Action taken		
		Male	Female	Verbal	Physical	Parents informed	Parents interviewed	Suspension

Pupil referral form

Pupil: **Tutor group:**

Lesson: **Date:**

Details: **For info. only** ☐

                                             I will consult:
                                             Form tutor ☐
                                             Head of Year ☐

Action taken so far:

                                                 Signed: _____

Form tutor: **Date:**

                                                   Signed: _____

Head of Year: **Date:**

                                                   Signed: _____

Form tutors may take further action or simply acknowledge receipt of this form *before passing to the Head of Year.*

Form tutors should, however, make the pupil aware that they have been informed.

The Pastoral Head's Handbook © Heinemann Educational Publishers.

Behaviour monitoring form

Pupil:

Form: Year:

Date	Details of behavioural problem/incident	School response	Parents informed

Pastoral review form

Year:		Head of Year:		Date:	
Pupil's name	Sex	Cause for concern		Agreed action	Review date

The Pastoral Head's Handbook © Heinemann Educational Publishers

Register of Concern and Special Arrangements

RB18

The Pastoral Heads Handbook © Heinemann Educational Publishers.

CODE OF PRACTICE SPECIAL ARRANGEMENTS/INDIVIDUAL EDUCATION PLANS

Year:

Date of issue:

Name	Form	Stage	Cause for concern	Arrangements/IEP	Review	Review	Review	Stage

Special Arrangements Report

Code of Practice Stage 1

Dear Parent/Guardian

It has been necessary to place your child on daily report to help improve his/her behaviour. Please check and sign the report every day. The report will also be checked daily by his/her form teacher.

Pastoral Head

Pupil: _____   Form: _____   Review date: _____

Please comment on the following: Behaviour/Attitude (additional comments can be made on reverse)

	Reg.	1	2	3	4	5	6	Staff signature	Parent's signature
Monday									
Tuesday									
Wednesday									
Thursday									
Friday									

This report should be completed and returned to _____ (Pastoral Head).

If problem behaviour occurs, please complete the section below.

Details of any problem behaviour (additional details can be given on reverse)

Date/lesson	What led up to the incident?	What happened?	What were the consequences?	Staff signature

The Pastoral Head's Handbook © Heinemann Educational Publishers

Individual Behaviour Plan and  Report

Code of Practice Stage 2

One form for each day of the school week.

Dear Parent/Guardian

Your child has been placed on an individual behaviour plan/report to improve his/her behaviour. Please check and sign the report every day. The report will also be checked daily by the Pastoral Head.

Name of student: _____

Tutor group: _____ **Date**: _____

Note: Would staff please tick if these targets have been met or put a cross if this is not the case, and add their signature. If problem behaviour occurs, please fill in the 'Details' section below.

Targets	1	2	3	4	5	6
1 To respond to any reasonable request made by a member of staff.						
2 To remain acceptably on task with work.						
3 To avoid 'shouting out'.						

Signature of Parent/Guardian: _____ Date: _____

Signature of Pastoral Head: _____ Date: _____

Details of any problem behaviour (additional details can be given on reverse)

Date/lesson	What led up to the incident?	What happened?	What were the consequences?	Staff signature

Contract for behaviour management

Code of Practice Stage 3

Date of commencement:

Date of first review:

Pupil's name: Date of birth:

Reasons for contract:

The School will:

_____ (Parents/Guardians) will:

_____ (Pupil) will:

Signed: _____ (Pastoral Head)   Date: _____

Signed: _____ (Parent/Guardian) Date: _____

Signed: _____ (Pupil)   Date: _____

The Pastoral Head's Handbook © Heinemann Educational Publishers.

Revised IBP Report

Code of Practice Stage 3

Name of student: _____

Tutor group: _____   Date: _____

Note: Would staff please tick if these targets have been met or put a cross if this is not the case, and add their signature. If problem behaviour occurs, please fill in the 'Details' section below.

Targets	1	2	3	4	5	6
1 To respond to any reasonable request made by a member of staff.						
2 To remain acceptably on task with work.						
3 To avoid 'shouting out'.						
4 To sit on own away from other pupils.						
5 To attend all lessons.						

Achieved all five targets: YES/NO

Signature of Parent/Guardian: _____   Date: _____

Signature of Pastoral Head: _____   Date: _____

Details of any problem behaviour (additional details can be given on reverse)

Date/lesson	What led up to the incident?	What happened?	What were the consequences?	Staff signature

Behaviour policy checklist

- What are the areas of concern shared by both staff and pupils?

- What sort of behaviour is most distracting or unsettling?

- Are procedures understood by all staff and pupils?

- Are sanctions consistently applied?

- Do pupils understand the sanctions and think they are fair?

- Does the school have effective ways of dealing with lower-level misbehaviour as well as major incidents?

- Does problem behaviour rapidly move up to the highest level of management or are there stages in the management of behaviour?

- Is the school actively monitoring and responding to all pupils' behaviour or is it just involved in crisis management?

- When and how are parents involved? Is it at an early stage of any concern or is it only when things are going badly wrong?

- Has the school got the balance of sanctions and rewards right, or is the ethos of the school punitive rather than encouraging?

- How widespread is any problem in the school?

- What do pupils think will make them behave well or work hard?

The Pastoral Head's Handbook © Heinemann Educational Publishers

Pastoral curriculum planning form 1 **RB23**

School aim	Values/beliefs	Topic	Activity

The Pastoral Head's Handbook © Heinemann Educational Publishers.

Pastoral curriculum planning form 2

YEAR:	TERM:				
School aim	Related pastoral curriculum aim	Week no.	Registration time	Assembly theme	PSE programme

The Pastoral Head's Handbook © Heinemann Educational Publishers.

Tutorial/PSHE planning form 1 (RB25)
– whole-school outline

Term	Wk	Year 7 Topic	Year 8 Topic	Year 9 Topic	Year 10 Topic	Year 11 Topic
ONE	1					
	2					
	3					
	4					
	5					
	6					
	7					
	8					
	9					
	10					
	11					
	12					
	13					
	14					
TWO	15					
	16					
	17					
	18					
	19					
	20					
	21					
	22					
	23					
	24					
	25					
	26					
	27					
	28					
	29					
	30					
THREE	31					
	32					
	33					
	34					
	35					
	36					
	37					
	38					
	39					
	40					
	41					
	42					
	43					
	44					
	45					

Tutorial/PSHE planning form 2 (RB26)
– room use planner

Term	Wk	Room: Year: Form:	Room: Year: Form:	Room: Year: Form:	Room: Year: Form:	Room: Year: Form:
ONE	1 2 3 4 5 6 7 8 9 10 11 12 13 14					
TWO	15 16 17 18 19 20 21 22 23 24 25 26 27 28 29 30					
THREE	31 32 33 34 35 36 37 38 39 40 41 42 43 44 45					

The Pastoral Head's Handbook © Heinemann Educational Publishers.

Tutorial/PSHE planning form 3 (RB27) – detailed plan

Date	Week no.	Lesson activity	Resources	Staff	Venue	Notes

Assembly planner

Month	Dates to note	Assembly themes	Readings/materials
Sept.			
Oct.			
Nov.	11th – Armistice Day		
Dec.	25th – Christmas		
Jan.			
Feb.			
March			
April	Easter ↓		
May			
June			
July	4th – USA Independence Day		
Aug.			

The Pastoral Head's Handbook © Heinemann Educational Publishers